The KFC Murders: A NEWS ACCOUNT
The deadly saga of the infamous East Texas 1983 KFC Massacre

The KFC Murders:

A NEWS ACCOUNT

The deadly saga of the infamous
East Texas 1983 KFC Massacre

Written by
Jacque Hilburn-Simmons and Kenneth Dean

Edited by
Richard Loomis and Melissa Loomis Wagner

DEDICATION

This book is dedicated to the memories of the victims, their families, area law enforcement officers, prosecutors and others touched by the murders. We also wish to thank our families, especially our significant others, Ray Simmons and Jennifer Piazza. Without their patience, encouragement and impartial wisdom, this book would not be a reality.

Table of Contents

Character Glossary

Ashley, Lynetta – Employee of Kilgore KFC
Avance, Marvin – Captain for Kilgore Police Department
Baker, Katie – Legal assistant to attorney Thad Davidson
Beasley, Lorna – DNA expert for Texas Department of Public Safety
Beene, John – Forensic scientist for Texas Department of Public Safety
Bennett, R. Daryll – Defense attorney for James Mankins Jr.
Brown, William – Investigator for Rusk County District Attorney's Office
Burks, G.W. – Captain with Texas Rangers
Clyde, Nelson III – Publisher of Tyler Morning Telegraph
Clyde, Nelson IV – Son of Tyler Morning Telegraph
publisher, current publisher
Collard, Doug – Crime scene commander for Tyler Police Department
Davidson, Thad – Defense attorney for Darnell Hartsfield
Dorsey, Leona – Girlfriend of Joey Johnson
Dowell, Stuart – Investigator for Texas Rangers
Downing, Nelson – Sergeant with Tyler Police Department
Duke, Keri – Property owner near crime scene
Dunkerley, Lana Maxwell – Wife of KFC employee, victim David Max-
well
Elliott, Glenn – Investigator for Texas Rangers
Ellis, Marvin – Reporter for Tyler Morning Telegraph
Ferguson, William – District Attorney for Rusk County
Franklin, Robert – Businessman who owned a white van
Freeman, Kyle – District Attorney for Rusk County
Giles, Dr. Robert – Genetic testing expert
Gist, Larry – State District Judge
Gossett, Clay – State District Judge
Gramm, Phil – Senator for State of Texas
Griffith, David – Defense attorney for Romeo Pinkerton
Haag, Lucien – Phoenix striation expert
Haas, Jeff – Defense attorney for Romeo Pinkerton
Hamilton, Kathy – Sister of KFC employee, victim David Maxwell
Hamilton, Fred – Stepfather of victim Joey Johnson
Hartsfield, Darnell – Inmate convicted of KFC murders
Headen, C.R. – Assistant Police Chief of Kilgore Police Department

Hughes, Jack – Husband of KFC employee, victim Opie Hughes
Hughes, Myra – Daughter of KFC employee, victim Opie Hughes
Hughes, Merle – Son of KFC employee, victim Opie Hughes
Hughes, Opie – Employee of Kilgore KFC, victim
Isaac, Jimi – Son of James Mankins Jr.
Jimerson, Micheal – District Attorney for Rusk County
Johnson, Joey – Employee of Kilgore KFC, victim
Johnson, Samuel – Witness in murder trial
Kieny, George – Retired FBI agent, investigator for Rusk County Sheriff's Office
Killingsworth, Don – Defense attorney for Darnell Hartsfield
Killingsworth, Leanne – Manager of Kilgore KFC
Landers, Monte – Fraternity brother of David Maxwell and Joey Johnson, victim
Landers, Linda – Mother of victim Monte Landers
Landers, Oscar – Father of victim Monte Landers
Mankins, James Jr. – Suspect in murder investigation
Mankins, James Sr. – State Representative, father of James Mankins Jr.
Maxwell, David – Employee of Kilgore KFC, victim
Maxwell, Donald – Father of KFC employee, victim David Maxwell
Maynard, Denise – Stepdaughter of KFC manager, victim Mary Tyler
McCarty, Mike – Officer for Tyler Police Department
Miller, Kimberly – Daughter of KFC manager, victim Mary Tyler
Monteagudo, Vincent – Private investigator, defense consultant
Morales, Dan – Attorney General for State of Texas
Nelson, J. Paul – Defense Attorney for James Mankins Jr.
Nicholson, Kersti – Brother of victim Monte Landers
Null, Robert – Witness in murder trial
Pinkerton, Romeo – Inmate convicted of KFC murders
Pirtle, Danny – Sergeant for Kilgore Police Department
Popps, Laura – Assistant State Prosecutor for Texas Attorney General
Reynolds, Wayne – Officer for Kilgore Police Department
Roby, Rhonda – DNA expert
Ross, Donald – District Judge
Rowe, James – Witness in murder trial
Ruby, Lenora "Lenny" – Acquaintance of James Earl Mankins Jr.
Shumate, Joe – Defense attorney for Darnell Hartsfield
Stanger, Harold – Principal at Overton High School
Stone, Dr. Irving – Forensic expert for Southwestern Institute of Forensic Sciences - Dallas
Strickland, Jerry – Spokesman for Texas Attorney General
Strong, Mike – Sheriff of Rusk County

Stroud, James – Sheriff of Rusk County
Tanner, Lisa – Prosecutor for Texas Attorney General
Turner, Bill – Criminal prosecutor, mentor to Lisa Tanner
Tyler, Billy – Husband of KFC manager, victim Mary Tyler
Tyler, Bob – Brother-in-law of KFC manager, victim Mary Tyler
Tyler, Mary – Manager for Kilgore KFC, victim
Williams, Doyle – Investigator for Rusk County Sheriff's Office
Winston, Elton – Friend of Tyler businessman Robert Franklin
Wolfe, Misty – Investigator for Texas Attorney General
Wright, James – Sergeant for Texas Range
Valadez, Manuel – Forensic expert, lab supervisor for Texas Department of Public Safety
Vasquez, Leticia – Spokesperson for Texas Attorney General
Warlick, Arthur – Oil Field Worker for Henderson Clay Products
Waters, Robert Lewis – Associate of Hartsfield and Pinkerton
West, Cecil – Officer for Henderson Police Department
Wiggins, Don – Lieutenant for Rusk County Sheriff's Office

Chapter 1
A Grim Discovery

East Texas oil field worker Arthur Warlick yawned and stretched as he shuffled into the kitchen for a final swig of coffee before heading to work.

He gazed out the window, liking the idea of an early start before the heat set in. If all went according to plan, it would take only a few hours to inspect the rigs and update the safety reports.

Warlick set down his cup, a stained remnant from an old country café, and strolled toward the back door, grabbing a well-worn straw cowboy hat on the way out.

Sunlight was just starting to peek through the thick curtain of pine trees as his old work truck bumped down the remote, narrow blacktop country road leading to his first stop.

It was Sept. 24, 1983, unusually crisp for this time of year, and Warlick's mind ping-ponged from work matters to the list of chores waiting at home, unaware of the horror lurking ahead.

He took a deep breath, savoring the freshness of the morning air.

Warlick scanned the tree line, hoping to glimpse the legendary buck that manages to dodge the bullets every hunting season, but there was no sign of the lucky beast.

Arriving at the first site, the lanky worker bailed out of the truck to unlock the gate and sighted several unfamiliar objects off the gravel road ahead, perhaps bags of garbage or debris from some pasture party.

"Little bastards," he said, swinging back into the cab. Pulling through the gate, he continued to peer at the objects as the truck eased forward.

Blasted trespassers, why can't they stay out? What did they mess with this time?

The back woods of Rusk County, Texas are perfect settings for mischief. Large areas are off the beaten path and difficult to access.

Warlick stopped the truck, shifted into park and climbed out.

He was angry. Somebody had to pick up the mess. It was blocking the road.

And if coyotes got ahold of the stuff inside, it could take the better part of a morning to pick everything up.

"I'm tired of this crap."

He reached for his work gloves and started walking up the gravel road toward the piles. Maybe it wouldn't take too long to get everything loaded. The cool air made his back feel stiff.

Warlick was watching his step so his boots wouldn't cause him to slip on the rocks.

By the time he glanced up, he was almost on top of the objects. That's when he realized the mounds weren't trash at all, but several people, apparently party-goers who decided to sleep it off in the field, thinking they wouldn't get caught.

Warlick couldn't see their entire bodies, only legs and feet sticking out of the tall weeds. Judging from the youngish-looking clothing, they appeared to be just kids, maybe college students.

No one seemed to realize he was standing there.

Tiny dots of perspiration erupted under his hatband.

He hoped this wasn't one of those group sex things.

Warlick stared in silence and embarrassment, debating his options: stay and interrupt their play time, or leave and return later, maybe after the kiddos sobered up and went home.

He rolled his eyes, imagining the laughing reaction of his co-workers. Yes, there would be no end to their teasing if he left to avoid an uncomfortable situation.

Maybe the guys were playing a joke on him, to see if he would go running scared.

Warlick's head jerked from side to side, scanning the dense tree line. Yep, they were probably hiding in the woods nearby – watching - waiting for an opportunity to jump out and scare him.

After a few moments, he decided play along.

"Hey, hey you kids," he said, his voice gruff for emphasis. "Y'all need to wake up now and get on home. You hear me?"

He took a few more steps and stopped, his faded work shirt fluttering in the morning breeze.

Something wasn't right. It was way too quiet.

Warlick cocked his head to listen, but heard nothing ordinary, no songbirds or the distant bawl of young calves pining for their mothers. Just wind blowing through the thick towering pine trees.

And why weren't those blasted kids gathering up their things to leave?

Warlick moved in for a closer look and grimaced. He caught his breath, his chest tight with shock and surprise.

Doubling over, he began to retch.

"My ... God."

The terrified worker whirled around and started running, almost tripping, in a panicked scramble for his truck CB radio.

"Hey, hey, I need help over here," he shouted into the microphone. "Please, please, somebody help me."

Chapter 2
Horror, Heartbreak

F ew Texas crime stories can rival the heartbreak, outrage and confusion associated with the decades-long investigation into the killings of five innocent people, referred to around East Texas as the KFC murders.

The saga of the infamous massacre is well documented in more than 30 years of archived interviews, stories and photos by journalists working for the Tyler Morning Telegraph and former partner publication, Tyler Courier-Times—Telegraph.

Their goal: to keep the story alive until the crime is solved.

The sensationalism of the execution-style killings gripped the small town of Kilgore like a vice, turning neighbor against neighbor as the primary suspect was vetted in the news media.

Investigating lawmen from various agencies engaged in a type of turf war over jurisdiction, prompting state and federal officials to join in, presumably to mediate and bring an end to the case.

Yet, more than 30 years have passed and the case remains open.

Public reaction to the finger pointing and snail's pace of the investigation was a mixture of disgust and rage – with so many resources, why was it so difficult to bring the murderers to justice?

From day one, the case was plagued with problems.

Warlick's message about his discovery in the oil field might have been directed at his supervisor, but it was broadcast to all radio listeners in the surrounding area.

The terrified worker was soon joined by others as well as a field supervisor, who alerted authorities around 10:10 a.m., unaware a feverish search was underway for the five people huddled together in the oil field.

Three fraternity brothers from Kilgore College and two working mothers had been kidnapped about 12 hours earlier from a Kentucky Fried Chicken in the nearby college town of Kilgore, Texas.

The restaurant was about 18 miles, give or take, from where they died.

Kilgore authorities already in the thick of the investigation theorized suspects forced their way into the restaurant after it closed for the evening, intending to rob those inside and then make off with the store's receipts.

But at some point in the scheme, things went wrong. A robbery turned into kidnapping and murder.

And Warlick's grim discovery seemed to confirm their worst suspicions.

Lawmen soon arrived in response to Warlick's call for help and found the slender asphalt county road leading to the oil field jammed with sight-seers, gawking and snapping photos.

"By 10:20, the whole country was full of people, helicopters and everything," a bewildered Warlick later told a news reporter.

Amid the chaos, several people ventured into the location for a closer look, trampling the grass in the immediate vicinity, forever disturbing key points of evidence for investigators.

In the initial confusion, no one thought to immediately secure the area surrounding the crime scene, which was soon overrun with lawmen from multiple agencies, some smoking and walking around the area to ease the tension.

Warlick's leathery hands were still shaking as he climbed

17

back into his truck and tried to comprehend the morning's events.

He watched the commotion as he waited to speak with an officer, trying to figure out the nature of the various activities and who might be in charge.

"They took my name and telephone number, but never said another word," he recalled.

He waited weeks for a call from authorities, but years would pass before he would be asked about the events of that morning.

By that time, the trail for the killers was stone cold and the town's people weary of waiting for justice.

Chapter 3
Vanished

The town of Kilgore, with boundaries that fall in both Gregg and Rusk counties, bubbles with excitement each fall as new and returning Kilgore College students – many away from home for the first time – test the limits of freedom.

Local police aren't generally fazed by their youthful antics, as the mischief and revelry is a far cry from some of the city's early bawdy days when it was caught up in the East Texas oil boom.

The discovery of the East Texas Oilfield in the 1930s marked the beginning of explosive growth in the area as people flocked there to seek their fortunes, swamping Kilgore's main streets with oil derricks, tents, shacks and ramshackle honkey-tonks before new laws helped restore order.

The expansive 140,000-acre field, in portions of Gregg, Rusk, Upshur, Smith and Cherokee counties, is recognized now as having the largest and most productive reserve in the United States, yielding about 5.2 billion barrels of oil from 30,340 wells.

The townspeople learned over the years to live with and accept the oil rigs, adopting them as a promotional tool for tourism and education.

On the night of the murders, 17-year-old Kimberly Miller was working at the Kentucky Fried Chicken in Kilgore, alongside her mom, Mary Tyler, 37, the restaurant's manager. Even though many of her friends were attending Friday night football games, the teenager was scheduled to work until 10 p.m.

As the minutes ticked by, she couldn't resist glancing at the clock. She was looking forward to a late night supper with her boyfriend before midnight curfew rolled around.

"Okay, I'm leaving," she told her mother and co-workers. "See y'all later."

Amid the excitement of clocking out for the evening, the girl forgot her money. Her date agreed to swing by the restaurant so she could borrow a little pocket cash from her mom.

They pulled into the restaurant parking lot around 10:45 p.m., just as Miller's stepfather, Billy Tyler, was driving up.

Billy Tyler met his wife while she was working at KFC in Longview and was smitten.

Mary Tyler was a pretty woman with dark curly hair and a wide smile. He appreciated her big heart and the way her blue-gray eyes twinkled when she laughed.

They soon married, pooling resources and energy to care for their blended family of five children, including Tyler's daughter, Kimberly, who had already been in trouble with the law, including a stay in a girls' home.

The 17-year-old's employment at the KFC came only after her mother assured top management she would pose no problems for the fast food chain.

"Hey, what's up?" the teenager called to her stepfather. "Where's Mom?"

When Miller clocked out at 10 p.m., her mother and co-workers Opie Hughes, 37, and Joey Johnson, 20, were still inside working.

Two of Johnson's frat brothers, David Maxwell, 20, and Monte Landers, 19, were also there, hanging out until the restaurant closed.

"Your mother didn't come home so I came to check on her," Tyler said, strolling toward the building.

Miller started banging on the front door, but received no response. Peering through the glass, the restaurant appeared empty.

"That's weird," the teenager said. "When I left, they were all in there."

They walked to the rear of the building and found both the back door and a second interior door open.

A bag of trash was by the back door, normally locked tight by that time of night.

Inside the restaurant, there was disarray: flour and cooking utensils strewn about, blood in the office area.

Someone's work cap was laying on the floor.

"Oh my God, what happened?" Miller said, surveying the mess. "Mom?"

"Maybe there was an accident," Tyler said. "Go call the hospital. I'll wait here."

Miller phoned Kilgore's Roy H. Laird Hospital to see if any KFC employees had come to the hospital for treatment of an injury, but the emergency room nurse said no one from the eatery was present.

The teenager asked her date to stop by the hospital anyway so see could check out the situation herself.

Finding no store employees, she phoned the restaurant and her stepfather answered.

"Daddy, they are not up here."

"No one's here either," he said. "Just me."

Miller alerted Kilgore Police that something was wrong at the restaurant – the place was a mess and several people, including her mother, were nowhere to be found.

Officers arriving at the location at 11:33 p.m. took a quick look around and realized they had a crime scene.

Chapter 4
Dreams Shatter

A few blocks away, Kilgore College freshman Lana Maxwell, 18, was at home on the couch, fighting sleep to keep her eyes open.

It was almost midnight and David Maxwell, her mischievous husband of nine months was late getting home, again.

The couple was still settling into their new apartment, an inexpensive, snug one-bedroom dwelling near campus, and Lana Maxwell was enjoying the adventures of turning the dated space into a home, for them and the tiny baby growing inside her womb.

The young woman enjoyed spending time with her husband and disliked the hours they were separated.

Lana Maxwell was crazy in love and, at the same time, terrified this newfound fairy tale existence – the opportunity to be a wife and mother – might be short-lived.

At the tender age of 18, she already understood the pain of loss.

Her 45-year-old father, a Vietnam War veteran, died of complications from alcoholism when she was only 10, leaving her mother alone and ill-prepared for the financial rigors of raising a child alone.

Mother and daughter subsequently became adrift in the world with little to call their own, except for stacks of bills and darkened rentals with disconnected water and electricity.

Life was hard, but the teenager was proud and knew she needed a plan to create a better life for herself.

She was careful to make sure to conceal the financial hardship so as to escape the judgment of her peers, relying on public restrooms for grooming and her smarts for avoiding child welfare authorities while her mother juggled multiple jobs.

The teenager enrolled in the spring semester of college while she was still in high school, so as to not lose her father's Social Security after graduation.

For a girl accustomed to living in unfamiliar hotel rooms, her tiny college dorm room at Kilgore College seemed like a palace and the tall, handsome, dark-haired young man she spotted at the end of the cafeteria table, a prince.

Having never had a boyfriend, she was smitten with the young man, introduced as sophomore David Maxwell, president of the college's Phi Theta Omega fraternity.

In spite of their dissimilar backgrounds – he was from a well-to-do local family – they hit it off immediately, staying up for late night poker in the boys' dorm and deep conversations that lasted into the wee hours.

In the days and weeks that followed, the couple became inseparable and married in a Christmas time wedding, barely a month after Maxwell proposed.

Lana Maxwell wore a borrowed wedding dress and the church was adorned with brilliant red poinsettias. Young and in love, they saw sunshine where in fact, evil was lurking.

Maxwell relinquished his plan of attending Texas A&M University and his role as fraternity president to marry, but ties with his Greek bothers remained strong.

Although he enjoyed his new role as husband and soon-to-be father, he still enjoyed hanging out with his buddies, drinking beer and playing poker.

The new Mrs. Maxwell frowned on his frat boy activities, but soon learned to appreciate some aspects of the brotherhood, starting with the day they misplaced their only set of car keys.

Joey Johnson, a sophomore in the Phi Theta Omega fraternity and one of Maxwell's closest friends, stepped up with an offer to share his motorcycle.

Although they attended different high schools, Joey and David had been friends for years. Both were high achievers and excelled in martial arts.

Maxwell was a former honor student at West Rusk High School, a member of the junior engineers' society and all-district band, said Principal Jimmy Jones.

Johnson was senior class president and "Mr. Overton High School," the highest honor awarded by the faculty.

Johnson lost his dad when he was a boy, but not before the father instilled the importance of a strong work ethic.

The teenager stayed true to his upbringing, playing multiple sports, even earning the distinction of membership in "Who's Who Among High School Athletes," said former Overton High School Principal Harold Stanger, who described Johnson as an "ideal student."

Johnson was as devoted in his personal relationships as he was a dedicated athlete. After the car keys were misplaced, Johnson and Maxwell agreed to take turns using the bike until the set could be found or replaced.

It seemed to be a reasonable solution for two guys who went to the same school and worked at the same place, the Kentucky Fried Chicken near campus.

Ultimately, that unlucky convenience was the reason Maxwell happened to be in the restaurant that night instead of home with his new wife.

And the lost set of car keys that served as the catalyst for Maxwell's death that night may have also kept her from joining him as one of the victims.

"Oh my gosh, I almost forgot," Maxwell said a couple of hours before he died. "I need to drop off Joey's bike; he's about to get off work."

Pulling a pair of dark gray coveralls over his cotton T-shirt and shorts, Maxwell looked at his wife and said, "Wanna go? It won't take long."

"Sure," she said. "Let me grab a jacket."

They climbed on the motorcycle and headed toward the restaurant, enjoying the cool Friday night fall air, one of the first breaks in the heat that season.

"Whoa, whoa, what am I thinking? We can't fit three people on here," Maxwell said, slowing the bike for a U-turn and a trip back home. "You stay here, I'll be back."

Lana Maxwell, excited about the open air ride with her new husband down the main drag, felt a wave of disappointment.

"Ok," she said with a pout, climbing off the bike. "Hurry back, I'll miss you."

She went back indoors and settled onto the couch to wait, thoughts drifting to her swollen belly and the tiny life within.

Sitting motionless in hopes of detecting a tiny fluttery kick, her eyes began to feel heavy and she struggled to stay awake. The clock read 11 p.m.

"Where is he?" she thought, feeling a flush of frustration as she snuggled back into a comfortable position.

Around midnight, she awoke again and went to bed angry, certain the guys decided to hang out and have fun without her.

Lana Maxwell was roused from sleep a short time later by Johnson's roommate, who stopped by the apartment and let himself in.

"Where's David?" he said flipping on a light.

"I don't know," she said blinking. "I thought he was with Joey."

The delay in returning home was out of character so they decided to stop by the restaurant to investigate.

Johnson's motorcycle was still in the parking lot, but there was no sign of either him or David.

Maybe the bike was broken down. Still, it wasn't like them to be away without explanation.

"I think we need to go to the police," she said.

The typically quiet Kilgore Police Department lobby was abuzz with activity. Authorities just received word from Tyler's daughter something was wrong at the restaurant.

"We can't find my husband and his friend, Joey," Lana Maxwell said. "They were at the Kentucky Fried Chicken."

"Wait right there," an officer said. "Don't go anywhere."

Moments later, she heard a voice from an interior office exclaim, "Oh my God, that makes five."

Chapter 5
The Evidence

A few miles from the restaurant, Kilgore Police Sgt. Danny Pirtle was making it a point to avoid the revelry of Friday night football.

It had been a hectic day at work. A quiet night at home seemed a perfect topper for a long week, filled with accident reports, lost pets and traffic citations.

Pirtle's only goal for the evening was to go to bed early, but the plan was about to change.

The weary officer showered and settled into bed, listening to the familiar tick-tick-tick of the ceiling fan whirling overhead. Peace at last.

Within minutes of settling in, his phone was ringing.

"Sergeant, you are needed at the KFC," the voice on the other end said. "Possible robbery."

"Hmm, okay," he said. "I'll be right there."

He sat up and stretched. Groggy with sleep, he forgot to ask for more details.

Fumbling with his clothing, he squinted at the clock. It was almost midnight. Minutes later, he was climbing behind the wheel and heading toward the restaurant.

"What the ...," he said, spotting a slew of officers at the location as well as the chief and other high-ranking administrators. "All of this, for a robbery?"

Pirtle's mind started racing as officers filled him in on what they learned to that point.

Officers found obvious signs of a struggle and blood splatters inside the restaurant. There were no signs of the employees or cash receipts.

A young restaurant employee reported her mother, the store's manager; and several others were missing.

There was also a frantic young woman in the police department lobby asking for help in locating her husband, David Maxwell.

The woman said he stopped by the KFC a few hours earlier and never returned home. One of his fraternity brothers, Joey Johnson, was supposed to be with him.

"Ok, let's get an APB out on these people now and send to every agency in the area," Pirtle said, his focus shifting to preserving whatever evidence remained at the crime scene.

Several people, including Miller and her stepfather, had already walked through the restaurant before police arrived.

Pirtle scanned the interior of the KFC, jotting notes.

The scene must be documented down to the smallest detail, including photos and fingerprints, in case the situation turned out to be more than a simple restaurant robbery.

Completing the tasks would take hours, even with a few sets of extra hands.

Pirtle hoped to receive a phone call indicating good news, but his optimism was fading fast.

The circumstances didn't look good. With each passing hour, the situation seemed increasingly dire for the missing.

Officers working inside the restaurant gathered for a word of prayer for the missing and their families.

If their worst fears were realized, the investigation would swamp the resources of the small town police department.

"I'll be back," Pirtle said. "I've got a really bad feeling. If this thing goes all to hell, we're going to need some more help."

His mind swimming with possible scenarios, Pirtle drove a few miles east to the neighboring town of Longview to seek help from someone with more experience in dealing with major crimes, Texas Ranger Glenn Elliott.

The veteran Ranger was well-respected among his peers and well versed on proper protocol for handling big crimes.

Smart, detail-oriented, patient, Elliott was a crackerjack officer who seemed to possess a type of sixth sense about solving crimes. When the action was hot, Elliott – tall in his crisp starched shirt – always seemed to be cool as a cucumber.

Elliott's law enforcement career began in 1949 as a state trooper and he climbed the ranks, becoming one of the elite Rangers in 1961 and staying in that role until retiring in 1987.

Pirtle knew he needed Elliott's expertise at this early stage in the investigation to help preserve the evidence and hopefully, come up with some leads.

It did not take much convincing.

Elliott listened during the younger officer's rundown of the few facts known about the crime.

"Sure, Danny, I'll be glad to help," he said, retrieving his gun and badge. "We'd better get going."

Upon returning to the restaurant, Pirtle started photographing the interior as other officers logged dozens of pieces of evidence and dusted for fingerprints.

He was already tired. He had been up for hours. His eyes stung, his shoulders felt like they were being squeezed in a vise, but there was no immediate end in sight to the documentation process.

As he slowly moved around the interior snapping images, he spotted blood spatters on a small box under the front counter and on the floor in the kitchen area.

The detective looked at the other officers and at Elliott.

"Looks like a pretty good fight happened here in the kitchen at some point," Pirtle said. "We've got blood in a few places, but nothing to indicate anyone suffered any major injuries here inside the restaurant."

"That's what it appears," Elliott murmured.

Flour blanketed the floor. Pots and pans were scattered like confetti.

No money was located in the store, but a suspicious indention mark was noted on one of the walls near the cash register.

"I think someone's head struck the wall right there," Elliott said, pointing so it could be photographed.

Pirtle spotted a small piece of folded notebook paper and, with gloved hands, picked it up - it was a love note to Joey Johnson, apparently from his girlfriend, Leona.

It must have fallen out of his pocket.

He read over the contents, but found it unremarkable, just chatty, lovebird conversation about their next date.

The investigator hoped the letter contained fingerprints of the suspects.

An eerie silence fell as the men studied the room, imagining the terrifying scene that played out here only a few hours earlier.

"Don't leave any stone unturned," Elliott said.

Every effort was made to capture the microscopic evidence left behind. Fingerprinting experts focused on dusting the dining tables, front counter, restrooms, windows, doors and any place a person could touch, although much of the surface area was already wiped down.

Outside the restaurant, there seemed to be a hundred set of eyes trying to peer inside.

The news media was camped near the curb, awaiting word on any story developments as police officials tried to field inquiries from local officials.

"Damn reporters. Why don't they go home?" someone said.

There was tremendous interest in the case and Pirtle understood why, at least from a local perspective.

In a small town, everyone seems to know everyone else, and their families, and their families' families, so there are deep personal connections.

"It's too bad so many people already came in through here," Elliott said. "It complicates things."

Authorities at the restaurant were still cataloguing evidence when Henderson Clay Products field worker Arthur Warlick made his gruesome find at one of his employer's drilling sites: five bodies, shot execution-style.

One of the victims was wearing a Kentucky Fried Chicken

uniform and nametag.

It wasn't difficult for the two police agencies to make the connection.

Pirtle shook his head after hearing the news, trying to make sense of it all. A mass murder, in Kilgore?

Things like this just didn't happen here.

Sure, Kilgore had its share of crime like any other town, but nothing that could compare to someone kidnapping and gunning down a bunch of college kids and two working moms.

"Them sum bitches," he said. "We're not letting those bastards get away."

Chapter 6
Every Cop's Nightmare

The bodies of the five people kidnapped from the Kilgore KFC were found in rural Rusk County near the area where Warlick grew up, outside tiny Henderson, Texas, home of the Heritage Syrup Festival that recalls the days when live mules ground corn into rich varieties of velvety, dark syrup.

In some respects, Henderson is a town that time overlooked. Buildings that predate the American Civil War still stand.

The city is generously populated with gracious historic homes, churches and landmarks that speak of its prosperous early days.

A quiet, humble man, Warlick preferred to live and work on the outskirts, enjoying his job that usually held little drama, except for that Saturday when he found the bodies.

Just a few hours before his horrifying discovery, stadiums across East Texas were alive with the sounds of Friday night football.

In a small town stadium outside Kilgore, cheerleaders from

West Rusk High School and Gilmer led a familiar cadence of cheers as football fans hooted and hollered in delight.

The smell of cheese nachos and hot dogs hung in the night air.

William Brown, 34, was among the officials running up and down the field watching for penalties.

He loved being a part of the game. It was a great way to unwind from stresses of his day job, that of serving Rusk County as an investigator with the District Attorney's Office.

Brown enjoyed watching the spectators almost as much as the game itself. It was refreshing to hear laughter and see smiling faces.

On the night of the murders, the panting referee's only care was not blowing a call and drawing the ire of the fans.

"Off sides," he shouted, blasting his whistle to the elation – and dismay – of the excited crowd.

He grinned, absorbing the excitement of the moment.

The elation was short lived. A few hours later, his life would be forever changed by one of the most infamous mass murders in state history.

Brown's involvement in the case began the next morning, as he was enjoying a first cup of coffee with his wife. The phone started ringing after only a few sips.

Assuming the call might be work-related due to the early hour, he responded with his customary greeting, "Yes, this is William."

He knew nothing about abductions in Kilgore.

"Sir, they've found five bodies," the Rusk County Sheriff's dispatcher said.

"What?" he said, head cocked in disbelief. "Say again?"

The dispatcher repeated the information: five people were executed overnight in a remote field off Walker King Road.

Brown put down the receiver and shook his head.

"Oh, what's wrong?"

"Bunch of people were murdered last night," he said. "I need to go see what's going on."

Questions began to crop up in his mind. Who were they, and why would someone want them dead?

He headed toward the bedroom to dress.

"Not sure when I'll be home, Hon," he told his wife a few minutes later, giving her a quick good-bye kiss. "Tell the kids I'll see them when I get back in."

On the drive out to the oil field, Brown was thinking about the killers.

They must be familiar with the area - it's far too isolated out here to stumble across by accident.

He spotted approaching cars and moved to one side of the skinny blacktop road to let them pass.

There seemed to be an unusual amount of traffic for a Saturday morning.

Nearing the murder scene, he realized the additional vehicles were no coincidence.

The area was crammed with motorists, sight-seers trying to catch a glimpse of the carnage. There were also helicopters hovering overhead and people milling about.

From a distance, the body language of first responders was telling – this was a bad scene.

"Damn it," he said.

Brown adjusted his Stetson hat, took a deep breath and climbed out of his Ford Crown Victoria, peppering nearby shaken officers with instructions.

"We need barricades," he said. "Quick - we've got to keep people away from here."

He saw weeds parted with meandering trails of foot traffic and frowned.

It didn't look good.

"Who's been walking through here?" Brown asked. "We need names and contact information of everyone who came through here."

They had just one chance to preserve the crime scene and establish a solid chain of custody for future prosecution.

His mind started clicking through crime scene protocol.

In an ideal situation, every footprint, broken blade of grass, blood spatter and bit of evidence at the site could be protected and documented for further investigation.

But this scene was far from fresh and Brown began worrying about how much evidence was already lost or compromised.

Chapter 7
A Killing Field

R usk County officers working to document the oil field crime scene quickly realized challenges in the case. Brown was still disturbed at the calamity around the scene and the audacity of nosy people to try and bypass authority.

There was little he could do about the aerial news coverage, but ground activities were another story.

The road remained busy with gawking passersby as the day unfolded. Some people attempted to approach on foot to sneak a peek at the murder scene.

"We've got to keep this place secure," Brown said. "Be sure to keep everybody back. We don't want anyone else in this area."

He made certain a log was established to keep track of everyone who entered the area and their purpose.

Officers fanned out to collect the names of people already connected to the scene, mostly oil field workers, who ventured near the bodies before authorities arrived.

"What's your name, sir?"

"Arthur Warlick."

"And the nature of your business here today?"

"I'm the one who found the bodies," he said, voice shaking. "I showed up this morning to check the gauges and found them laying there. I thought someone was trying to play a joke on me or something, but it wasn't a joke."

The officer shook his head as he jotted down a few notes and collected the frightened worker's home phone number.

"Thank you, sir. Someone will be in touch."

Brown was standing nearby, taking an overall look at the area surrounding the crime scene and reviewing the facts as he knew them.

The road running adjacent to the oil patch was remote with few houses.

A slender, thread-like gravel road extended from the road to the oil pumping site.

The bodies were found in the weeds just off the road - three young men and a woman laying side-by-side; a fifth person, a female, was several yards away. The gate leading into the site was closed when Warlick arrived.

Brown scanned the bodies and detected signs of injury – small sections of their hair and clothing was tinged with dry, dark blood.

Though no one could tell for certain until they were autopsied, it appeared each victim was shot more than once.

Investigators could see that one of the young men, later identified as Joey Johnson, seemed to have multiple shots.

Neighbors also reported hearing the sounds of late-night gunfire, which was unusual considering it wasn't yet time for deer hunting season.

The victims' pockets, turned inside out, were empty.

The investigator surmised the killers must have pulled up to the gate and, finding it locked, forced the people to march up the dark road to their deaths.

How could they see?

There were no nearby streetlights, little traffic and few homes.

At night, the dense woods seemed to morph into a sea of dark nothingness, making it difficult to see a hand in front of your face much less a gravel road leading to an oil site.

Brown knew the moon had been nearly full, but would that have been enough light to illuminate the area?

Maybe the killers parked at the gate and turned on the headlights, blinding the victims as they tried to look back toward the main road.

If so, maybe neighbors saw headlights, maybe a vehicle description.

Brown studied the bodies, troubled by their positions. No one seemed to be in a defensive position as if doubled up in fear.

The victims were all face down, but no one had their nose stuck in the dirt.

Instead, their faces were resting on their crossed arms, as if waiting for the kidnappers to bolt to their vehicle and speed away.

"They might have been told to lie down and wait," Brown said to no one in particular. "They might have assumed they would be able to get back up. They might have been told if they cooperated, they wouldn't be hurt."

Had they realized death was coming, they would be fighting like hell to escape.

Their bodies would be scattered about the field, not lined up in an organized formation.

It was a cruel, remorseless way to murder, like shooting fish in a barrel.

Still, there was the issue of that one woman, Opie Hughes, found separate from the rest.

Attired in a brown and beige work uniform with red and white athletic shoes, her body position was different from everyone else.

She was also face down, but in a more defensive mode, clutching tight fistfuls of dirt and weeds.

Did she figure out the deception and try to run?

No matter what unfolded in those final, awful moments, these poor people didn't deserve to die like this, in the dark, in the middle of the woods.

Brown fought to refocus his thoughts. The cool morning air was being replaced by a heavy humidity more typical for

September in Texas.

There was no time to waste.

"It's heating up," Brown said. "We've got to wrap this up. We need these bodies to be in good condition ... they are probably our best evidence."

The officers worked fast to locate, record and preserve anything that could prove useful in the investigation.

"Get 'em bagged," Brown said. "Let's go."

Investigators placed paper bags over the hands and feet to protect forensic evidence that might be on the body or under the nails.

Each body was placed into a large black bag for transport to the Dallas Medical Examiner's Office. An officer was instructed to travel with the victims to preserve the chain of custody.

With the bodies removed, attention turned to the ground beneath them.

"We need to locate the bullets," Brown said. "Let's be sure we don't miss anything."

"Yes, Sir."

Investigators began sifting through the sand, using small screened trays to recover any bullets or fragments.

Further away from the murder scene, other officers – some on horses or ATVs - fanned out in search of other evidence.

Others tromped shoulder-to-shoulder through high weeds and dense plum thickets searching for anything out of place.

Nothing went unchecked: every fresh candy wrapper, soda bottle and cigarette butt was flagged as evidence and collected for forensic testing.

No one knew if the items belonged to the oil field workers or the suspects.

Trained search dogs tried to catch a whiff of the suspects while other lawmen used ATVs and horseback to access more remote areas.

It was an arduous task and everyone was soon physically and emotionally drained. The lawmen were human, after all, and everyone had families of their own.

Brown found himself haunted by his own imagination.

He kept thinking about the victims and how frightened they

must have been on that long, last drive from the restaurant into the dark woods.

They probably huddled together, terrified and in shock, while other people were sitting in stadiums, cheering their favorite football teams.

It just didn't seem fair.

Under ordinary circumstances, Brown would be home, scanning the newspaper for the scores of Friday's game between his beloved Texas Aggies and Oklahoma State. Coach Jackie Sherrill and the Aggies had needed a Friday win, but A&M lost, 15-34.

Instead of perusing football scores, he was staring at a line of dead people, cut down in the primes of their lives. People who had Saturday routines, just like him.

Brown's mind churned, pondering the possibilities and searching for an explanation.

Many weeks would pass before his mind would clear enough to enjoy a game of football.

Chapter 8
Lives Interrupted

S omewhere on a long stretch of highway outside Kilgore, worried truck driver Jack Hughes was racing toward home.

He was out of town working in Box Spring, Texas, when his wife, Opie, a night employee of the KFC and mother of three, didn't make it home from work.

Hughes learned of his wife's absence from his children, who relayed word that something was wrong and he was needed at home right away.

"Mama didn't come home last night," the small, frightened voice on the other end of the phone said.

Hughes was frightened and concerned. Opie was a petite, kind-hearted, devoted wife who would never stay away from her family without good reason.

He rolled back into Kilgore hoping for good news, but there was still no official word on her whereabouts.

Hughes stared at his wedding band, a match to the one he slipped on her finger that hot July day in 1963. He was 20, she was 19.

It wasn't like her to be a cause of worry for the family. Where was she?

Hughes arrived home and found little to do but wait. As he looked out the window, he sighted a lone figure approaching the house. It was a police officer.

Hughes fought back tears as he opened the door. Their eyes met and Hughes knew, even before the officer said a word, his precious wife would never walk through the door again.

Lana Maxwell was seeking comfort in the company of her in-laws when word emerged five bodies were found in Rusk County, but she refused to buy into the idea he was gone.

David was a prankster and she was certain he and his buddy, Joey, would burst through the doorway at any moment with a funny story to tell. She was sure of it.

"Lana," her mother-in-law said. "They are calling for five body bags."

The tearful young widow phoned her mother, who lived in Longview. The 58-year-old woman had no car, but started walking the estimated 10-mile stretch to Kilgore in a desperate bid to reach her daughter.

A couple of hours later, a police officer spotted the exhausted woman nearing town and gave her a ride.

Chapter 9
A Gentle Boy

Among the five people found murdered was Kilgore College freshman Monte Landers, a graduate of Gladewater High School and a pledge in Maxwell and Johnson's fraternity.

Monte Landers had just moved into an apartment near the college. He popped by the restaurant around closing time to see his friends and got caught up in the robbery.

Landers' family, who lived out of town, didn't realize he was among the missing until they heard his name announced on the radio after his body was discovered in the oil field.

His stunned mother, Linda, a social worker by profession, sank into a chair at the kitchen table.

"It's got to be someone else," she cried, eyes welling with tears.

The German-born Monte, his given name Montegomery Louis Landers, was her oldest child, a gentle-spirited, outdoorsy boy who loved rodeos, karate and fast sports cars.

In a moment of boredom, he would grab his mom and they would dance together in jest, whirling around and around up to the point of dizziness.

At 19, Landers enrolled in Kilgore College with the intention of someday becoming a forest ranger. The family was excited when he began talking about being a pledge in Maxwell and Johnson's fraternity.

"Please, somebody do something," Linda Landers screamed. "They can't be talking about our Monte."

Her husband, who helped with maintenance at a nearby university, tried to calm her fears.

"We'll check this out, Sweetheart," he said. "Maybe it's a mistake."

The family prayed for a miracle, but the ugly truth was confirmed Sunday after a visit with the authorities.

It was a crushing blow for the close-knit family, which included Landers and four younger siblings, including a set of twins set to graduate from Pine Tree High School the following spring.

Monte's mother screamed and fell to the ground, her anguished cries echoing through the house.

There would be no last dance.

"I will never again feel those skinny arms or hear that laugh," she said through tears. "I will never hear him say, 'I love you Mom.'"

And just like that, the humble life the family loved – the summer vacations, playful sibling bantering, Sundays at church – was changed forever.

Landers' younger sister, Kersti, 17, who also heard the radio announcement, crawled into bed with her mother that first night – as well as many others - in hopes of quieting the heart-wrenching sobs, but there was no easing the suffering.

The family was haunted by the knowledge that their Monte, the soft-spoken Christian son who refused to watch horror films, would experience a nightmare in his last moments.

Kersti insisted on returning to high school Monday morning to attempt an escape from the crushing sadness at home.

An awkward uneasiness hung in the air as she entered the bustling school hallway.

Classmates spoke in hushed tones, their stares averted as she passed.

Teachers dabbed away tears.

Her closest friends surrounded her in a protective cocoon, but there was little they or anyone could do to ease the pain that would continue for the rest of her life.

Chapter 10
Mr. Right

West Rusk cheerleader Leona Dorsey went to bed happy and woke up screaming.

She was in love with victim Joey Johnson, believing he could be her "Mr. Right" and partner in building a better life.

They met one night on Commerce Street a few months before the murders in the small town of Overton, Texas, a rural community of about 2,100 people.

On the night they met, Dorsey was chatting with friends when a young man with a big grin and a motorcycle pulled into the parking lot and rolled up to where they were standing.

"I paid no attention because I didn't know him," she said during a 2014 interview. "I said something about being bored and this red-haired guy offered to take me for a ride on his motorcycle. I gave him a dirty look and told him I don't ride off alone with guys I don't know."

Her father had long cautioned her that good Christian girls should act "hard to get" so boys will stay interested and pursue them instead of the other way around.

Dorsey relented and accepted the ride after friends assured her Johnson was a gentleman and could be trusted. She was careful to touch his waist with her fingertips and not sit too close. They puttered around Overton for a while and Johnson returned her to the parking lot, safe and sound.

The pair ran into each other a few weeks later, at the same parking lot, as Dorsey and several girlfriends were on their way to a friend's birthday party.

"Leona Dorsey!" Johnson called. "Where have you been? I've been looking all over for you. I've called I don't know how many Dorseys I found in the phone book. I called Kilgore, New London, Overton, Arp, Troup ... where do you live?"

"Henderson," she said with a grin.

Dorsey was flattered. She wasn't very popular at school because she was more of a scholar than a partier. She was a member of the National Honor Society, first chair trombone in the band and a thespian in One Act Play.

Dates were rare, so when Johnson, a college boy, showed an interest in taking her out, he got the cheerleader's attention.

They had a lot in common, each was one of eight children in their respective families.

Money was always difficult to come by, but the stigma of living in poverty didn't matter because it was a bond they shared.

Dorsey was cheering at the West Rusk-Gilmer football game the night Johnson was murdered.

The Gilmer Buckeyes won, as usual. After the game, she went home and fell asleep listening to the radio and thinking about her new love.

A chilling announcement on the radio roused her from Saturday morning slumber: Five people had been kidnapped from a Kentucky Fried Chicken and murdered in a Rusk County oil field.

"No," she screamed when the location of the restaurant was disclosed. "Joey works at the Kentucky Fried Chicken in Kilgore!"

She ran into her parents' bedroom, hysterical.

"Wake up!" she begged. "Please, please, I need the keys to

the car."

The three dressed and raced to Johnson's home, but found no one there.

There was no answer at the neighbor's house either, so the trio sped to the Overton Police Department.

The sole person at the location, a dispatcher, wouldn't confirm that Johnson was among the victims and instead phoned the city manager, who rushed to city hall to meet them.

The city manager guided the family into his office and confirmed the unimaginable: Johnson was among the dead.

Horror-stricken, Dorsey ran out of the office and out into the street, screaming and crying until she collapsed. Her father rushed to her side, almost crushing her in a tight, tearful embrace.

"Sweet Daddy," she told the newspaper in 2014. "He tried to console me."

But there would be no shelter from the awful truth for the girl or any of the others affected by the murders.

Chapter 11
Families Struggle

In the days following the murders, there was simply no escaping details of the KFC murders in East Texas.

It made front page headlines, the victims' faces highlighted in print and on television.

For the families of the deceased, the ring of the phone – invariably someone expressing sympathy or a reporter seeking information – kindled the raw emotions of it all.

There was little relief from the pain or the attention, said Landers' sister, Kersti Nicholson, now a mother of three.

More than three decades later, she is still moved to tears over her family's difficult struggle to find normal again after his death.

"Daddy tried to shield us a lot, he tried to protect us," she said. "He didn't want us bothered by anyone."

She's haunted by what her brother must have felt in his final moments.

"I know he was incredibly frightened," she said, as tears trickled down her cheeks.

Maxwell's father, Donald, who died in December 2001, told the Tyler Morning Telegraph in 1983 he desperately tried to cope with his grief by helping investigators search for personal effects of the victims that were stripped away in the robbery.

He made daily calls to authorities in hopes of learning something new.

"It's extremely frustrating," he said. "You want to do something, but you don't know what to do … probably the most tragic thing with something like this is, if it were an accident, we could bury them and start over. Now, it will go on until it's brought to a successful conclusion."

Bob Tyler, whose sister-in-law Mary Tyler, was among the victims, told the newspaper his brother struggled to cope with the guilt that survivors sometimes feel after the loss of a loved one.

"Billy usually picked her up, but he had to work that night," Bob Tyler said.

Within days of the murders, a group calling itself "Outraged Citizens of Kilgore" raised several thousand dollars to aid families of the victims.

A special fund was set up to aid Johnson's mother and surviving siblings. At the time of his murder, Johnson had been working to help support the family and put himself through college.

Other money was raised to benefit the expectant Lana Maxwell, who found herself broke and unable to cover the apartment rent.

Kilgore firefighters, upon hearing about her dilemma, volunteered to move her belongings to a small mobile home near friends.

She reluctantly accepted the offer, weeping as she gathered up her dead husband's clothing, hugging the items on the way out the door.

"It smelled like my David," Lana Maxwell Dunkerley, now a Houston businesswoman and grandmother, said in a 2013 interview. "I just buried my face in those clothes, I was missing him so much. I just couldn't believe he was gone."

Chapter 12
Details Emerge

T he Dallas medical examiner's office would soon relay some initial autopsy findings: four of the victims were shot twice; Johnson, three times.

Any one of the wounds was severe enough to cause the death of the victim.

Reports conducted Sept. 25, 1983 at the Southwestern Institute of Forensic Sciences indicated Hughes sustained a gunshot on the right side of the head behind the ear and a second to the back of the neck.

Tyler was shot first in the back from a distance with a second close range shot to the back of the head, but other injuries, such as those suffered by someone during a severe beating, were noted as well on the autopsy:

"A red contusion measuring 1 by from ¾ to ½ inch is located on the back of the left shoulder, a linear contusion extends 5 by 1/8 inches diagonally along the left side of the back from midline to the axilla. A small blue contusion is located on the left breast laterally. A tiny abrasion is noted on the left ring finger which has an impression of a ring."

No jewelry was found on her body.

Was it Tyler who was thrown against the wall?

Maxwell suffered two shots to the back of the head, one upper, one lower; while Landers was shot twice in the back of the head, once on the right side, according to the autopsy.

Johnson sustained a shot to the back of the head at close range, plus a shot to the neck and the right side from a longer distance, the report states.

Brown was intrigued by the overkill on Johnson. Why was that boy shot more times than everyone else? Maybe he tried to put up a fight or tried to run.

The medical examiner also reported all five victims tested negative for drugs and alcohol.

Authorities needed to learn more about the victims. Who were they, and why would someone want them dead?

One of the witnesses questioned during the early hours of the investigation was Dorsey, 16, whose love note to Johnson was found at the restaurant.

A detective questioned the girl to collect her thoughts and fingerprints, the latter to confirm she was the love note author and see if the killers handled the note.

"Leona, sweetheart, we want to see if there are any other fingerprints on the note, other than yours and Joey's. Does that make sense?" the detective said. "Good. Now, what can you tell us about the last time you saw Joey?"

Dorsey, dabbing her eyes with a tissue, told authorities she last saw her boyfriend on the afternoon of Sept. 23, 1983, a few hours before he died.

He surprised her by dropping in at her high school with an invitation for lunch. She accepted the opportunity to leave campus for a while and climbed on the back of his bike.

"I was on top of the world riding a motorcycle with Joey down 42 at lunchtime to the store instead of going through the line at the cafeteria," she said. "We sat on the stone pillars in front of the school and ate and talked and laughed like we always did when we were together. When it was time for me to go to class, I sure didn't want to go."

But she remembered what her father said about playing hard

to get and she decided to return to class instead of playing hooky. The detective nodded and Dorsey continued.

"I did mention to Joey that since it was Friday, I would be cheering in the pep rally that afternoon and wondered if he might be able to come back and watch me cheer," she said. "He said he would try. That afternoon dragged by so slowly, I couldn't get him off my mind. I even wrote him a note while I was in Mrs. McCathran's English class. It really wasn't astonishing, I just wanted him to know I was thinking about him. Sure enough, he made it to the pep rally. He watched me cheer and I was on top of the world. It was such a wonderful day for me."

"That's good," the detective said. "What happened next?"

Dorsey said her boyfriend stayed around after the pep rally and they chatted until it was time for her to get ready for the Gilmer football game.

"I gave him the note and he put it in his pocket," she said, crying at the recollection. "I wanted to invite him to the football game, but it was out of town and I was afraid he might have to tell me he couldn't go. I would be cheering all night and in the band at halftime, so I wouldn't get to spend that much time with him, even if he could get there. I think he had already told me he had to work anyway. I sure was hoping to see him again the next day, though, on Saturday. I thought about him that night at the football game."

The girl seemed unaware that her boyfriend didn't have use of his motorcycle that evening because he loaned it to Maxwell.

"Do you know if Joey ever used drugs or if anyone might want to hurt him?"

No, came the response, everybody loved him.

"Joey was the most popular guy at Overton High School," she said. "He was class favorite all four years of high school. He was a star athlete in football, track, baseball and weight-lifting and I don't even know what else. He was even elected Mr. Overton High School."

Authorities kept the original love letter as evidence, but Dorsey was given a copy for a keepsake.

Investigators received similar impressions of the other victims. The five appeared to be decent, hard-working people who got caught up in a bad situation and were killed.

Back at the oil field, it took almost a week to recover the last of the bullets from the area where the bodies were located. There were 11 in all.

The last one recovered, described simply as a "large caliber," was discovered with a metal detector. All were sent to the Department of Public Safety office in Tyler for examination.

Just when it seemed meaningful progress was being made in the investigation, the unthinkable happened: critical evidence was destroyed.

The city of Kilgore had been trying to operate within a tight budget and it was decided that film development could be done cheaper in-house at the fire department rather than sending it out to pay retail.

Pirtle dropped off his film from the restaurant crime scene and waited anxiously to review the shots.

He had been careful to document even the smallest detail, snapping away through almost a dozen rolls to help record the scene.

When he went to retrieve the prints, there was a certain uneasiness among fire department personnel.

He was handed a single envelope with a handful of photos.

"Where's the others?" Pirtle asked. "There should be a lot more."

"Danny, something happened in development and the rest were ruined," came the reply. "We're really sorry."

The investigator stared at the small stack of photos, his head swimming in disbelief and horror.

They had just one opportunity to document the crime scene and there was no going back for do-overs.

The photos were gone forever, never to be seen or recreated. How could the case be solved without them?

He thought of the victims and their families and the killers still out there, free to strike again.

Pirtle cringed at the anticipated fallout and shook his head. He wanted to throw up.

"Oh, my, God," he said aloud. "What are we going to do now?"

Chapter 13
Hunting for Killers

As the search for the KFC killers continued, the town of Kilgore, known for oil derricks, friendly faces and an award-winning college precision drill team, was caught up in an ugly spotlight.

Citizens were terrified for their children's safety. Rewards of $50,000 were posted, asking for information that could lead to the arrest of the killers.

Many public schools in the area halted their practice of allowing high school students to leave campus for lunch. Some people stopped visiting fast food outlets out of fear the killers might strike again.

As suspect leads began pouring in from around the region, lawmen started compiling a list of names and chasing what seemed like endless trails in the quest for new information.

Rusk County Sheriff Mike Strong was eager to solve the case, even if it meant speaking with a psychic to generate productive leads.

"Let's just say it's being considered," the sheriff said.

As wire services picked up word of the psychic, Rusk County investigator Doyle Williams publicly denied the agency summoned the supernatural assistant in an official capacity.

"Some psychics have given me some good leads, but I never really came up with anything," Williams told the newspaper, recalling assistance from an earlier case that didn't yield leads. "That case had gone cold and she gave me a bunch of stuff to work."

Stress and exhaustion soon set in for lawmen, sparking a type of territorial turf war among agencies.

Authorities in Kilgore were probing the robbery and kidnapping while investigators in Rusk County were trying to solve the murders.

The early spirit of cooperation soon cooled and information exchanges between Kilgore police, Gregg and Rusk County Sheriff's offices, became less frequent.

The public wanted answers. Why hadn't there been any arrests?

The bickering and finger-pointing eventually became so nasty, the Texas Rangers sent in two officials, Capt. G.W. Burks and Sgt. James Wright, to help coordinate efforts between the two counties.

Authorities attempted to downplay the necessity of the intervention.

"Having a coordinator will maintain a cohesiveness between the two investigations," Kilgore Asst. Police Chief C.R. Headen said. "I think it will expedite the process."

Texas Ranger Stuart Dowell wasn't sure what to make of all the commotion and tried to steer clear of it.

He was a tall, no-nonsense lawman in a white Stetson. He had quiet demeanor that garnered respect when he entered a room.

The Ranger, who was assigned to Rusk County, entered the investigation shortly after the bodies were removed from the crime scene and he attended the autopsies at the Southwest Institute of Forensic Sciences in Dallas.

Dowell was out of town for training when the bodies were discovered and returned to find a full blown, multi-agency investigation already underway.

Like the other lawmen, Dowell was anxious to round up credible leads that could lead to arrests and he soon had his first break.

As Dowell was helping the medical examiner undress Johnson for autopsy, they observed a jagged fingernail fall out of the waistband of the young man's blue jeans. The nail appeared as though it had been ripped away from the rest of the nail.

"Well, look at that," Dowell said. "That's interesting."

"Isn't it?" came the response.

The fingernails of the five victims were examined, but none appeared to have a missing nail tip, although Tyler did have an injured nail.

Tyler's autopsy noted the discrepancy as well as other injuries:

"Fingernail clippings are obtained from the left hand and a broken nail from the right. None of the clipped nails nor the remaining short nails show any similarity to the torn fingernail recovered from the clothing of victim 2632-83."

Dowell decided the nail could have come from one of the killers so he began contacting people on the suspect list, hoping one had an injured fingernail.

One of the people on the list was Kilgore resident James Earl Mankins, Jr., a sort of local outlaw with a seemingly insatiable appetite for drugs.

The suspect's father was James Mankins Sr., a former Democratic state representative who owned Ace Transportation trucking company in Kilgore. The younger Mankins worked as a driver and knew many of the back roads in East Texas like the back of his hand.

The elder Mankins, who died in 2013, was considered by many a pillar of the community. He represented Gregg County in the Texas Legislature for five terms, starting in 1975. He was a tail gunner in World War II, civic philanthropist and longtime church leader.

He always worried about his son, who was addicted to street drugs.

The younger Mankins was already under police scrutiny as word broke about the killings.

Longview police arrested him the day of the murders for unlawful carrying of a weapon after officers found him with a handgun and a rifle.

He was bailed out of jail and investigators soon discovered he had borrowed yet another handgun from an acquaintance in Gregg County and returned it the day after the murders.

Investigators received word Mankins was making statements around town some people found disturbing.

"We'd better bring him in and have a little talk," Dowell said. "He's been talking strange, telling people things like, 'If you cross me, you'll end up like the Kentucky five.'"

"That's pretty telling," a detective said.

Mankins agreed to meet with investigators at the Rusk County Sheriff's Office to put to bed any suspicions about possible involvement.

It was in that Oct. 1, 1983 meeting with Mankins that Dowell noticed something unusual that would set the tone of the murder probe for the next decade.

The middle finger of Mankins' right hand was injured and the tip of his fingernail missing.

"Jimmy, what happened, how did you hurt your finger?" Dowell asked.

Mankins was aware the Ranger was staring at his hand.

"I don't know, I just caught it on something."

"Well, do you mind if we make a cast of it, to eliminate you as a suspect?" Dowell said.

"Sure, why not?"

Mankins denied having any part in the murders and was eager to help prove his innocence.

Authorities created a mold of his finger for a plaster cast to compare with the fingernail recovered from Johnson's clothing.

There were some physical likenesses in thickness and striation of the two, and Dowell was convinced he had his man. He just had to prove it, starting with the elimination of other possible suspects.

There were dozens of people to interview, about 56 in all, including two cousins from the neighboring city of Tyler, Texas - Darnell Hartsfield and Romeo Pinkerton, according to the original list drafted by authorities.

Dowell continued working down the list, but his attention never left Mankins.

The Ranger questioned Hartsfield in November 1983 while he was in custody at the Smith County Jail in Tyler for a Sept. 26, 1983, aggravated robbery and burglary of a habitation.

Hartsfield, at the time of Dowell's visit, was no stranger to Tyler police.
The cash-strapped young man was always on the lookout for an easy way to gain a little pocket money.

The Tyler Food Store at 917 S. Vine St. seemed to be an easy target for Hartsfield and his buddy, Robert Louis Waters, to score some cash without much effort.

The lone female employee at the counter was busy tending to store business when the men entered, Hartsfield brandishing a .38 caliber pistol.

"Give me the cash."

The cashier didn't put up a fight, allowing the pair to make off with about $300 in assorted bills and the satisfaction of knowing they could soon replenish their supply of weed.

The robbery was not the smartest of moves. The timing, just three days after the KFC killings, captured the attention and imagination of a public still reeling from mass murders in their own backyards.

Tyler, recognized as the Rose Capital of the United States and the birthplace of football great Earl Campbell, is not immune to crime. But the city's residents much prefer to read headlines about its robust economy and high employment numbers, instead of possible mass murder suspects running the streets.

Tyler police acted swiftly after the convenience store holdup to help calm a jittery public.

Authorities had suspicions on who might have carried out the crime. An arrest warrant was issued for Hartsfield after a witness picked him out of a series of police mug shots.

Meanwhile, Kilgore authorities chasing leads to the KFC murders took note of the Tyler robbery and wanted to learn more, based on the possibility the two violent crimes could be connected.

"They've got a history of robbery," Headen, Kilgore's assistant police chief, said, explaining the rationale for wanting to question the men, known for hanging out in his town and in the Longview area.

Kilgore police issued a bulletin, asking any law enforcement agency that came in contact with Hartsfield, Pinkerton and a third man, Elton Winston, 29, to alert them at once.

Part of their motive in speaking with the men may have come from a witness statement collected around 12:40 a.m. Sept. 24, 1983 from KFC employee Kimberly Miller, just hours after the five victims were reported missing.

Miller, who clocked out just before everyone disappeared, told police she observed a man who seemed to be eavesdropping on a phone conversation with her mother, who called to check in with the employees.

In her statement to police, Miller wrote:

"On Friday, 9/23/83 at approximately 7:30 p.m., my mother called the Kentucky Fried Chicken and wanted to know how we were doing. I told her we had run $1,300. Standing at the counter was a black male, approximately 25 years of age, about 6' tall, 180 pounds. He had a clear plastic cap over his hair, he had a full beard and a mustache. On the right side of his face was deep pits in his skin, approximately three or four. He had on a gray T-shirt and tennis shoes and faded blue jeans. This black male watched me when I opened the register. Approximately 10 p.m. on 9/23/83, David Maxwell, a man that works there, and a man named Monte W/M, who are friends of Joey came to the front door of the restaurant when I was walking out and my mother let them inside and she locked the door."

Kilgore PD's bulletin seeking contact with the suspects set off a blizzard of inquiries from area news media that caught Tyler police off guard and put them on the defensive.

Tyler authorities had been working on the sly to find Hartsfield, dropping by area clubs with his photo in hopes of grabbing him before he went into hiding.

At least that was the tactic up until Kilgore authorities put out the word the trio was wanted for questioning.

Tyler police declined to say the men were linked in any

way to the murders, but did acknowledge it was reasonable Kilgore police would have an interest in questioning them for crimes in their city.

A frustrated Tyler Police Sgt. Nelson Downing tried to temper the furor.

"We were looking for him (Hartsfield) for one aggravated robbery," he said. "No one was hurt, no shots were fired."

Along with the .38 caliber pistol used in the robbery, Hartsfield was known to carry a .357 Ruger Blackhawk and drive a borrowed white van. He could also have a cut on the arm.

Authorities probing the KFC murders knew linking the suspects to the killings could be difficult, unless someone started talking and admitted their involvement. There was no physical evidence and DNA discoveries were in the future.

The men were later located, questioned and cleared of any involvement in the murders, but their brushes with the law continued.

By November, however, both Hartsfield and Pinkerton were behind bars at the Smith County Jail – Hartsfield for the convenience store robbery; Waters, for violating his parole for an unrelated aggravated armed robbery charge.

While the pair was incarcerated, Waters confided to another inmate he and Hartsfield were the ones responsible for robbing and murdering the people from the KFC, but the inmate said nothing to authorities about the conversation for 18 years.

As the years passed, the nail sliver and plaster cast taken from Mankins' finger would be examined over and over with mixed results. Some experts claimed it was a match while others said it was not.

A frustrated Rusk County District Attorney William Ferguson said on the five-year anniversary of the slayings there was little that could be done with the case without something more tangible.

"I know when there is not a case," he said. "The evidence we have is not sufficient to obtain or support a conviction."

The fingernail and other critical evidence from the crime scene was packed away and preserved in hopes that one day, a guilty conscious and or advances in science would surface, generating a break in the case.

No one could know for certain if the items might someday lead to a conviction, but the evidence would be waiting.

Chapter 14
State Steps In

I n the 1990s, the state's 48th Texas Attorney General, Dan
Morales, was trying to boost political traction and gain the
public's confidence as a man who could get things done.

He served from 1991 through 1999, during which time he
helped orchestrate a $17 billion settlement with big tobacco
companies.

Morales agreed to take over investigation and prosecution
of the stalled KFC murder case in November 1993 at the request of former Rusk County District Attorney Kyle Freeman.

The cold case was so complex and voluminous, the county
prosecutor's office did not have sufficient resources to work
the case and then take it to a jury.

The charismatic, talkative Morales enjoyed the spotlight
and knew that if his office could successfully prosecute the
infamous mass murder case, his star would shine bright in the
state's capital.

Maybe Texas voters would remember it when the time came
one day to select a new governor.

Morales agreed to spearhead a new look at the case, which

hinged largely on the stray fingernail found in the waistband of victim Joey Johnson during autopsy.

Up to that point, much of the attention on Mankins seemed to center on his repeated run-ins with local law enforcement over drug and firearms offenses, including an arrest the day of the murders for unlawfully carrying a weapon.

Mankins always seemed to be in and out of jail, but in 1985, he was sentenced to serve three years of federal time for using the phone to distribute and sell methamphetamine.

After Morales took over the KFC case, hopes of progress began to reawaken.

A special grand jury was convened to begin hearing from possible witnesses and reviewing related evidence in the case.

Morales met with the families of the victims to assure them of his resolve to seek indictments and then called a news conference to let the public know his office was bent on bringing the killer or killers to justice.

The families "waited long enough," he declared.

"Our job is to ensure that justice is done," Morales said. "Our job is to ensure the grand jury has an opportunity to review all relevant facts, all relevant evidence – scientific, testimonial and otherwise – and that is what we are doing."

Morales said his assistants, just in the brief time his office was involved, had already logged thousands of hours preparing the case.

The state was sparing no effort in bringing closure to the case, giving his assistants access to the state-of-the-art scientific and medical advances, which would make it possible to overcome the age of the case.

"I believe an indictment could be returned, and, ultimately, convictions could be had, based on evidence that is available," the attorney general said. "We have placed the best prosecutors, the best investigators we have available in our agency, on this case."

Relatives of the victims seemed relieved the cold case, which had languished more than a decade, had not been tossed to the wind.

They expressed hope the grand jury would find enough evidence to indict.

"We're glad they're not giving up on us," David Maxwell's widow, Lana, told the newspaper.

The state began issuing subpoenas to compel testimony from those with possible first-hand knowledge about the kidnappings and murders.

There was intense public interest in the unfolding developments and the press seemed eager for any scrap of information coming out of the confidential March 1995 grand jury proceedings.

Much of the attention was still focused on Mankins Jr., one of about 20 people responding to the subpoenas.

The Tyler Morning Telegraph published the witness list, which included some of Mankins' known associates, friends and family as well as investigators and scientists.

Among the parade of witnesses was Lenora "Lenny" Ruby, nicknamed "Tiger Lady" for once possessing a large Bengal tiger, said she was happy to testify.

Ruby said she knew the junior Mankins well and even picked him up from jail the day of the murders after he was jailed on the weapons charge.

She said she cooperated earlier with authorities to keep her drug selling operation up and going.

Ruby said Elliott didn't shut down her drug sales so long as she agreed to turn over any guns, jewelry and other items that could be linked to the KFC murders.

Elliott denied the woman's claim, saying he did not observe the illegal sales, but reported unlawful activities to the proper authorities.

Other witnesses included victim Mary Tyler's daughter and husband.

The victims' families, emotionally drained, remained hopeful.

"We're taking it one day at a time now," Maxwell's widow said. "This is just the beginning. We've gotten kind of numb at this point, but we'll know something at the end of the week."

Mankins' attorney at the time, J. Paul Nelson, was unsure why the state was going after his client and questioned its motivation in doing so.

"I don't know what they (Texas Attorney General's Office) are doing or what they think they will accomplish, but certainly, like everyone else, I believe if they've got something they need to do something with it," the attorney said.

The elder Mankins also took to the airwaves to defend his son, claiming he was innocent of the murders and law enforcement was chasing the wrong man.

The following month, more than a decade after the murders, the news families had been waiting for arrived.

Morales stood outside the Rusk County Courthouse and announced that a KFC grand jury on April 27, 1995 handed up five capital murder indictments against Mankins, who had already turned himself in to authorities.

The indictments came as a relief not only to the families, but also to lawmen, who found themselves together again for a single cause. They were elated at the development, but still cautious.

Retired FBI agent George Kieny attended the news conference and studied the reactions of the various family members, who seemed overjoyed with progress on the case.

"I'm real happy for them," he said, satisfaction in his voice. "I can see a lot of relief in their faces."

Kieny came out of retirement to work as an investigator for the Texas Attorney General's Office and help out in the case.

He wanted to fully retire, but simply could not walk away from the job, leaving East Texas' most heinous crime unsolved.

He hoped fate was on their side.

"Anybody that's ever worked on the thing has got to be extremely pleased with the point we arrived at today, no doubt about it," Kieny said. "But there's still a lot of work to do."

Brown was also present at the news conference.

"I'm elated," he said with a grin. "We've waited a long time to see somebody go behind bars. We've crossed the first bridge. We still have a long way to go."

Rusk County Sheriff Cecil West, who was a police officer with the Henderson Police Department when the murders occurred, said a huge burden was lifted when indictments were handed up.

"I feel great myself," he said. "I feel like it's a weight lifted off this office and probably the district attorney's office as well."

West said the agencies that investigated the crime learned a lot from the experience, and the extent of collaboration was much improved.

"I feel like that was one of the hindrances early on, a lack of cooperation, and now we've got total cooperation between all the agencies involved," West said. "I think that's finally what brought it together is cooperation."

Authorities set a high bond, $2.5 million, or $500,000 for each charge, in hopes of keeping Mankins behind bars.

The indicted suspect, dressed in an orange jail inmate jumpsuit, pleaded not guilty to the charges before District Judge Donald Ross.

R. Daryll Bennett, a tenacious cigar-chomping defense attorney, stepped in to represent Mankins.

He argued for a bond reduction, claiming his client lacked the assets to raise the minimum amount necessary to hire a bail bondsman.

The judge disagreed.

But Bennett wasn't about to throw in the towel. He appreciated a good challenge and wasn't afraid to acknowledge it to the world.

"Son," he quipped to a Tyler Morning Telegraph reporter. "A grand jury can indict a ham sandwich, but that don't make the sandwich guilty."

Mankins also addressed the court, admitting to previous convictions for alcohol, drug and weapon offenses, but denying he was violent or abusive, citing, as an example, his willingness to cooperate with authorities.

At the bond reduction hearing, Rusk County Sheriff's investigator Lt. Don Wiggins and Pirtle testified about what they saw at the crime scene.

Brown described the positioning of the bodies and Dowell testified he was present when the fingernail fell out of Johnson's waistband.

The Texas Ranger said two striation experts, Dr. Irving Stone from Dallas and Lucien Haag in Phoenix, indicated the fingernail appears to have come from Mankins, based on comparisons with the cast.

The court was also advised the Southwest Institute of Forensic Sciences sent the nail to Genescreen in Dallas for testing.

Dr. Robert Giles said Genescreen technology at that time was helpful in narrowing the field of possibilities for a match.

Bennett said the screening techniques used as a basis to indict his client were "speculative" at best and he pushed for more definitive, sophisticated testing and a change of venue.

The defense attorney also filed dozens of pre-trial motions to try and exonerate his client, including one seeking expert assistance in DNA testing on a bloody napkin that was said to come from the restaurant.

The motion indicated an analysis of the blood on the napkin during the initial investigation revealed a blood type different from Mankins.

Then Rusk County District Attorney Bill Ferguson agreed to seek the opinion of Herbert McDonald of Corning, N.Y., a well-known striation expert who testified in the O.J. Simpson trial.

A change of venue was also granted, allowing all five charges against Mankins to be moved to Jefferson County.

About 50 pounds of case files arrived ahead of the trial, surprising the office staff.

State District Judge Larry Gist, seeing the arriving mountain of paperwork, was concerned about pretrial publicity.

He issued a gag order to ensure Mankins received a fair and impartial trial that was not prejudiced by a "circus atmosphere."

In his order, the judge hinted he might bar live television coverage, if either the prosecution or defense objected to the presence of cameras in the courtroom.

"I am sensitive to and concerned about public dissemination of improper information," the judge wrote. "It is my firm intent to try this case professionally in the courtroom and not in the media. I am committed to seeing that each of you receive a fair and impartial trial. I intend to do everything in my power to ensure that a circus atmosphere does not occur either inside or outside of the courtroom."

However, neither the defense nor the prosecution opposed the idea of being on television.

"We won't make any objections to televised coverage of the trial, but we will ask the judge to make some guidelines so cameras won't be in the way to fall over and jurors are not distracted by them," AG spokesperson Leticia Vasquez said.

For a time, everyone was so focused on taking Mankins to trial, it seemed unlikely anything could derail it.

Then came the unexpected.

Attorneys received the results of new, more sophisticated DNA tests conducted on the fingernail: Mankins was not a match.

Bennett felt a wave of relief and reiterated his position that Mankins played no part in the murders.

"He (DNA expert) looked at the nail twice, once for federal prosecutors, and once for Bill (Ferguson)," Bennett said. "Both times he said it was not a match. We had pictures of the nail looked at by our own expert in Portland, Ore, who said even by the pictures there was no way he could say positively the nail identified Jimmy or did not."

With no other definitive evidence linking Mankins to the murders, Gist dismissed all five charges against him.

Bennett downplayed the likelihood of second indictments, saying the prosecution had no more evidence against Mankins.

He said it was time for authorities to look elsewhere for the real killers and leave his client alone.

"Now that it's been proven it's not his nail, I think all this talk about Jimmy, unless there is some concrete evidence, needs to stop," Bennett said. "I'm not saying the investigation needs to stop. I'm saying it needs to stop as far as accusing Jimmy. In my opinion, this exonerates him."

The normally quiet Mankins also issued a public statement, expressing his condolences to the families.

"Nothing I can ever say to you can convince you that I did not take the lives of your loved ones or that I have no idea who did," he said. "Twelve years of rumor and innuendos against me can never be erased from your mind by anything I can now say or do."

Mankins' son, Jimi Isaac, said afterward his family was relieved the ordeal was coming to an end.

"I'm glad it's over," he said. "It's been real hectic on our family and real hard on our father. These rumors have gone on for 12 years. I've heard the rumors, but we have got to keep our heads high and go on with our lives."

Kathy Hamilton, Maxwell's sister, said she was shocked by the development, but expressed confidence that Attorney General Morales would keep his promise and bring closure to the case.

"We are more committed now than ever to solve this," she said, touching five "tribute bracelets" on her wrist. "I know the attorney general's office is redoubling its efforts ... I don't want people to forget who the real victims are here."

Morales, humbled by the public dethroning in the case, vowed to continue seeking a resolution, but little progress was made before he left office.

The state's top attorney did eventually appear before a jury - not to try and resolve the KFC murders, but to defend himself against charges levied against him. Those stemmed, in part, from the earlier flagship tobacco settlement he helped negotiate.

Morales was convicted of falsifying documents to divert in excess of $500 million in settlement money to another attorney for supposed legal fees.

In 2004, the disgraced former prosecutor was sentenced to four years in a federal prison in Texarkana for mail fraud and filing a false income tax statement.

In an unexpected twist, he was sent to the same federal prison where Mankins was serving time on charges unrelated to the KFC case.

Chapter 15
The Long Wait

As the KFC murder case began to grow cold, families fuming for justice relayed their frustrations to the local news media.

The Tyler Morning Telegraph and Tyler Courier-Times—Telegraph newspaper, products of the family-owned T. B. Butler Publishing Co. in Tyler, was among the loudest critics, using its opinion and editorial space to call into question the apparent lack of progress in the investigation.

Leading the charge was Publisher Nelson Clyde III, a traditional newsman and civic philanthropist, who liked a good crime story.

Clyde grew up in the news business, the heir apparent to a daily paper that prided itself on accuracy and thoroughness.

He was born Nov. 1, 1945, in Tyler to Calvin Nelson Clyde Jr. and Patsy Elizabeth Clyde, working his way to the top of the family business to become the fourth-generation publisher.

Clyde started out as a paper delivery boy, learning the ins and outs of what it takes to get a freshly printed newspaper into a driveway before dawn.

He was a well-educated, analytical man, who insisted that his reporters chase a story until they caught it.

In his later years, after becoming the boss, he ran the newspaper from a small glass-walled publisher's office overlooking the newsroom.

Sometimes he would pause from his work and stroll through the rows of reporter desks to check on stories in the works.

When a hot topic came along, Clyde never seemed to tire of examining the issue from every angle.

He wanted the last read on controversial stories and didn't hesitate to phone a reporter himself to discuss his concerns, even as it was nearing 10 p.m. press deadline.

Clyde was willing to hold the presses to make sure critical stories were to his liking. It was, after all, his newspaper.

And so it came to no one's surprise when Clyde took a personal interest in the KFC murders. He wanted justice for the victims and knew from chats with the newspaper's sources the case was going nowhere, fast.

A year after the slayings, the Tyler Courier-Times--Telegraph took up the charge, firing off an eight-column headline that said: "Kilgore Killings: An Open East Texas Wound."

The story featured the voices of anguished family members, including Oscar Landers, whose son Monte was among the dead.

"I think they've screwed up," he said. "I think they know who did it and I don't know what the holdup is."

Operations Editor Marvin Ellis, also a veteran newsman, was among those enlisted by Clyde to help keep the story alive and in the public's eye.

On the four-year anniversary, Ellis penned an opinion column quoting sources close to the investigation.

"The case started on the wrong foot, and from comments from many officials, it has not improved," he wrote, also citing remarks from an FBI agent, who mused, "It's such a big mess ... they have really bungled this one."

Ellis conducted numerous interviews to chase down information and check out rumors. He visited inmates in prison and met confidential sources in faraway places to learn new information, then reported his findings back to Clyde.

In 1989, Ellis again penned a commentary, lashing out at the apparent lack of progress.

"Rumors surfacing over the years include police going on wild goose chases, guns reportedly used in the killings disappearing and the death scene not having been secured," he wrote. "The Rusk County Sheriff's Office found it had no case file after a change of administrations last year and had to obtain one from other sources. Early in the investigation, the Department of Public Safety was called by Rusk County District Attorney Bill Ferguson two weeks following the murder to help 'coordinate the investigation' because of law enforcement in-fighting. A Ranger captain was sent from Dallas, but it really did not help, adding more frustration. So much bickering was going on between departments, no consolidated effort was possible."

Unbeknownst to the public and even law enforcement, the newspaper was tunneling ever deeper into a frightening underground criminal network of killers and drug pushers.

There were rumors the murders were drug related.

Dowell believed a recipe for methamphetamine was believed hidden in the restaurant, but it disappeared, angering the drug makers. The recipe was said to produce meth of such high quality, it was almost worth its weight in gold or diamonds.

The Ranger believed the people murdered happened to be at the wrong place, becoming casualties of a drug operation gone awry.

Clyde recognized the seriousness of the rumors, so extra steps were taken to check out each new bit of information and the sources behind it.

The newspaper also invested in a polygraph expert to administer lie detector tests to those being quoted, to distribute only factual information to the reading public.

As the days and weeks passed, the newspaper assembled an expansive array of information, including the original suspect list created by authorities, crime scene photos, scientific test reports, recorded interviews, personal correspondence and other documents.

During this time, the newspaper published a photo of the bodies at the crime scene, angering the families.

Clyde felt compelled as a newsman to hold people with the power to make a difference accountable for the lack of progress.

He wanted justice and believed the shocking images of those photos would pressure authorities to keep digging for answers.

Eventually, the stress of the open investigation began to take its toll on the newsman.

Fearing for the safety of himself and his family, Clyde added security precautions at both his and Ellis' homes. He had a security system installed at his home and he started taking different routes to and from work.

The newspaperman also began confiding in his son, Nelson Clyde IV, then a freshman in college, and explaining the various facets of the story as well as its many players.

It was the first time Clyde ever shared background information about a story with his son, but he was becoming too concerned to keep his work a secret any longer.

Their first talk unfolded during a long drive, when it was just the two of them in the car.

"Son, it's important to me that you know some things that we've found out about KFC," the elder Clyde said. "This story is a lot bigger than anyone realizes."

The younger Clyde didn't understand at first why his father wanted to talk about work, but it started to make sense. He realized the strange tone in his father's voice was there for a reason.

"Dad, do you think they would come after you?" he asked, aware of a sudden feeling of unease. "Is that why you're telling me this stuff?"

There was a long pause before Clyde finally answered, weighing his words so as to not alarm his son.

"I'm telling you this because I think it's important for you to know what's going on," he said.

Other talks followed, each with the acknowledgement that the newspaper could pull back at any time, but chose instead to remain on course.

Rather than take a step back, the paper continued monitoring and publishing developments in the case as they arose, including watchdogging the various court appearances.

Much of the press centered on Mankins, who was in and out of courtrooms fighting drug charges, alongside allegations of mass murder.

The newspaper was careful to ensure the families had a voice.

When it appeared progress was being made in the case, Johnson's grief-stricken mother, Kathryn Hamilton, commemorated the occasion by wearing one of her son's shirts from his days in a one-act play at Overton High School.

"We're getting something done … it's been hard to wait," she told the newspaper. "I'll always be angry. It's something you can't get over. I don't know why it took so long."

Her husband, Fred Hamilton, agreed, adding, "I hope this (progress) can begin the healing process for my wife. I sure hope so."

Chapter 16
A Bombshell

I n 2002, the newspaper worked with its confidential sources to publicize the fact that new DNA testing helped authorities link three suspects to the murders.

Those results indicated trace evidence found at the restaurant and on one of the victims belonged to black males.

However, Mankins, the longtime suspect, was white.

Furthermore, two of the assailants were known to the criminal justice system, meaning their DNA was already logged into the database; the third was not.

Clyde knew the news would be a bombshell for a public anxious for answers.

He summoned a handful of editors and a reporter to his personal downstairs conference room to update them on the latest development.

Setting a large black binder and stack of yellowing files on the conference table, the newsman reminded the group of the events leading up to that day.

"I've been speaking with one of our informants," Clyde

said. "They have apparently identified suspects through DNA testing, but the DA down there is not ready to do anything about it. People need to know what's going on with this case."

The binder contained documents critical to the investigation – copies of the suspect list, court filings, autopsies, crime scene diagrams – amassed over the years.

Clyde arranged for a series of interviews so people tied to the investigation could better explain the break in the case to his staff.

"We are the only ones who know about this," Clyde said. "I don't want anyone talking about it in the newsroom. No one is to know until we are ready to move forward with the story. Understand? Not a word."

Within days, the newspaper ran a front page story announcing the DNA findings, setting off a renewed firestorm of criticism over continued delays in the KFC murder investigation.

Authorities refused to acknowledge the revelation in the case and Rusk County Sheriff James Stroud lashed out at the newspaper for saying so.

Stroud said the newspaper was wrong in reporting the information before authorities were ready to move forward. He never said the information was inaccurate.

Stroud demanded to know who leaked the information to the newspaper, but journalists maintained the confidentiality of their sources, digging deeper into the story and paying visits to prison inmates who had been contacted about the case.

Authorities responded by issuing subpoenas to compel the journalists to turn over their notes and testify before a Rusk County grand jury, but the newspaper and its attorneys fought back, asking a judge to quash the motions.

The newspaper was successful in protecting the identity of its most valued informants and keeping its reporters out of the witness seat.

Frustrated family members continued speaking out.

The elder Mankins entered the fray, writing a letter to the newspaper in 2003 complaining about the lack of progress and continued scrutiny of his son.

"You would think after 20 years, with the expertise of the Attorney General's Office, Rusk County Sheriff's Office, past

Texas Rangers and other law enforcement officials, something would have come of this case," he said.

As one example, he cited an excerpt from Elliott's book, a Ranger's Ranger: "... there was one thing people either did not know, or chose to overlook – in 1995, we did not have one shred of evidence that we did not have in 1983."

Mankins' letter addressed Elliott's statement, saying, "... no telling how much money has been spent, nothing to show for their effort. I hope it doesn't take 20 more years to prosecute the ones actually responsible for those murders."

Clyde died in 2007 at the age of 61, leaving his son to take over as publisher as the investigation entered a new phase and one of the suspects was about to go to trial.

For the current publisher, continued coverage efforts seem to be as much about keeping the story alive as paying tribute to his father's desire to see all the killers behind bars.

Until that happens, the headlines will continue, Nelson Clyde IV said in a 2013 interview.

"From our standpoint, we can't wait until the story is finished," he said. "We feel like it is our responsibility to follow this case until the last person responsible for the killings is behind bars."

Chapter 17
DNA Breakthrough

A t the same time the victims' families anguished over their losses, a spunky young lawyer at the Texas Attorney General's office was learning the ropes by investigating and prosecuting child sex crimes.

Attorney Lisa Tanner hated the horrors suffered by the young victims, but enjoyed the challenge of snaring monsters.

With each new case, she felt increased gratitude her childhood in the tiny Texas town of New Caney was relatively normal.

She was an athletic country girl, who enjoyed dogs, wide open fields and the squealing pigs she raised as a project for Future Farmers of America.

Tanner never considered a career in law, but after landing a scholarship to study agriculture economics at Texas A&M, she fell in love with the rules of parliamentary procedure and later parlayed those interests into post-grad work and a law degree from Baylor University.

The rookie attorney's toughness, attention to detail and

growing track record of wins soon impressed the bosses at the Attorney General's office, especially a higher up veteran prosecutor, who summoned her into his office one day to extend an offer she couldn't refuse.

"Have a seat," he said, adjusting his leather chair so that it faced her. "You've been doing some good work here and it hasn't gone unnoticed."

The young attorney enjoyed visiting his office because it provided an opportunity to soak up a little history: walls filled with framed newspaper clippings, trial photos and thank you letters spanning decades of practice; bookshelves, an eclectic mix of law books and smiling family photos.

Tanner respected him and hoped the purpose of their meeting was to discuss a pay raise.

"Thanks," she said. "I really like it here."

"You know Lisa, we've been talking and we want you to take over KFC," he said. "We think you can do a good job on that case like you did on the others. You interested?"

Her face started to burn; so much for the pay increase.

"Hell no,'" she said with a grin. "Why that case, what did I ever do to you? Give me one good reason why I would want that case."

"Because," he said, looking over his glasses, "if you don't take it, we'll have to send it back to the DA."

He was teasing, of course, and Tanner knew it, but she didn't want to entertain the idea of giving up, even in jest.

She was intrigued by the idea of poking around the cold case, especially one that seemed so bungled.

More than a decade had passed since the murders and everyone in the office knew the case was besieged with problems: no chain of custody, few photos, a lost evidence log, a messed up crime scene.

In spite of having been on the job only two years, Tanner was the obvious choice because she was the only person out of the six-member office who had prosecuted a case based on DNA evidence, having just wrapped up her first case only a few weeks earlier.

She was still weighing the possibilities when she realized her boss was still waiting on an answer.

"Well?"

"Ok," she said. "I'll take it … but I'm not sure why."

By late afternoon, as the first wave of case files began arriving in her office, Tanner reached for the Tylenol.

"Good Lord," investigator Missy Wolfe said, rounding the corner and almost walking into a stack of boxes. "They aren't wasting any time on this one."

Wolfe was Tanner's right hand around the office. The veteran investigator was smart, insightful and meticulous.

She enjoyed difficult cases and viewed the decades-old murder case as an intriguing challenge.

"This will be interesting," Wolfe said.

"To say the least," Tanner said. "At some point, after we sort through this mess, we're going to have to explain it everyone else."

The women started peeping into boxes in search of a reasonable place to start.

Numerous officers from multiple agencies had their hands in the investigation over the years, and there seemed to be no end to the hundreds of file folders. In fact, there were so many records an entire room was allocated to them.

As the boxes continued to arrive, Tanner began to worry that no matter how hard she and Wolfe worked on the case, earlier missteps in the investigation might keep justice just out of reach.

For years, many people believed Mankins was responsible for the murders, based on visual similarities between his injured finger and the mysterious fingernail found in the victim's clothing.

He was indicted for the murders, but state prosecutors who took over the case from local authorities knew superficial likenesses weren't enough to convict and more conclusive testing was warranted.

DNA tests later conducted on the fingernail were found to be inconclusive.

"We need something more concrete," Tanner later told her boss during another of their office sit-downs. "It's like we're having to run down a bunch of damn rabbit trails to find something useful."

"So let's keep looking," he said.

At that time there was one option for more sophisticated testing on the fingernail – the former Armed Forces Institute of Pathology, which specialized in the collection of pathological specimens for medical evaluations, but is now closed.

Federal officials at first declined to participate in the KFC investigation, prompting the Texas Attorney General's office to seek assistance from Texas lawmakers Phil Gramm, Sam Johnson and other influential associates, who peppered the agency with help requests.

Federal examiners eventually agreed to examine the nail using a combination of micro photography and digital analysis, reporting in October 1996 the tiny sliver of fingernail everyone thought belonged to Mankins belonged to Mary Tyler, one of the victims.

Tanner called the news her "oh crap" moment – putting her almost back at square one on the case, which had been entirely focused on Mankins.

"This is probably the worst moment of my career," she said, reaching again for the Tylenol.

"We'll get through this," Wolfe said.

As the women resumed their search for new leads, DNA experts at the Texas Department of Public Safety lab in Garland, Texas, decided to do their own probing.

The lab still had custody of the original blood evidence recovered from the restaurant in 1983 so forensic experts decided to test the items and see if advances in technology could help pinpoint the suspects.

In 2001, Lorna Beasley performed DNA typing on the box and napkin then entered the data into Combined DNA Index System, known also as CODIS.

The system identified two Texas prison inmates, Darnell Hartsfield and Romeo Pinkerton as being at the restaurant. Hartsfield's DNA was found on a product box; Pinkerton's on a rumpled napkin.

The results also excluded Mankins as having a role in the murders.

Both Hartsfield and Pinkerton were on the first suspect list several lines under Mankins' name, but they had what seemed to be airtight alibis at the time.

However, DNA said something else.

Tanner's mouth dropped when she received the news.

"Oh my God," she said. "Those guys have been there all along."

It was time to update the families. A comfortable hotel conference room in Tyler provided a neutral gathering spot for Tanner to update the victims' families, yet there was noticeable tension in the air.

"I'm here today to tell you that basically, what you've known for 20 years was wrong," she said, laying an old "information wanted" poster on the conference room table.

The flyer, created just days after the murders, featured Polaroid snapshots of Hartsfield, Pinkerton and a third man, Elton Winston.

"What's that?" someone asked.

"We have DNA evidence on those two men," Tanner said, pointing to Hartsfield and Pinkerton.

One woman began to sob. Several people became angry and refused to believe that Mankins was not a player in the murders.

It was Jack Hughes, still grieving the loss of his wife, Opie, who was among the first to come around.

"Okay," he said. "Where do we go from here?"

The prosecutor cautioned the families that justice would not come overnight and urged them to remain strong, as there were many loose ends to tie up.

Tanner and Wolfe decided in 2001 to start back at the beginning and take a fresh look at each victim's clothing to seek out random stains or anything that could have been overlooked, such as a suspect's blood.

Tanner, in a 2013 interview reconstructed the conversation on the day she and Wolfe took another look at the evidence.

She said they spread each set of clothing out on a large table for closer examination. The room was quiet as they looked at the various items, still soiled, bloody and frozen in time.

When they reached Hughes' work uniform, the women noticed something.

"That's weird," Wolfe said, pointing out an unusual stain on the woman's bra. "What's that doing there? That's not sweat or deodorant."

"Hmmm, I don't know," Tanner said. "Let's look at her panties."

Wolfe dug around in the bag, but found no undergarment. Assuming it might have been misplaced they looked at the medical examiner's report, but there was no mention of it.

"That doesn't make sense," Tanner said. "She was wearing polyester pants. She's not going commando in polyester."

"You don't think she was sexually assaulted do you?" Wolfe asked.

They examined the crotch of the pants and noticed some discoloration, apparently overlooked in the earlier investigation.

"That could be semen," Tanner said.

Kieny was also in the room.

"She may have had sex earlier in the day," he said. "That could belong to her husband."

True, Tanner said, but no one could be sure without first checking it out.

Wolfe took the clothing to Tyler police, who used a forensic light to confirm the presence of body fluids such as semen and blood.

The pants were taken to Garland the next morning to the Texas Department of Public Safety DNA lab so the substance could be identified, maybe pinpointing sex and race.

Tanner suspected the tests would indicate that the semen belonged to either Hartsfield or Pinkerton.

She felt confident that convening a grand jury could help develop a chain of custody and record for prosecution. Both suspects could be brought in to testify.

Tanner believed there was enough evidence to indict Hartsfield, even though the DNA results from tests on Hughes' slacks were not yet back from the lab.

In her mind, she began planning the best way to announce the development when Beasley phoned from the lab and announced yet another twist in the case.

"I have good news and bad news. We have almost a full DNA profile from the semen."

"What's the bad news?" Tanner asked.

"It doesn't match anybody," Beasley said.

Tanner decided to hold off on the indictment and instead work with Wolfe to learn the identity of the man whose semen was found on the slacks.

Hughes' husband was ruled out early on, so efforts turned to collecting DNA from other sources, primarily from people summoned to testify before one of four grand juries considering evidence in the case.

Sometimes witnesses were simply asked if they wanted to submit a DNA sample so that they could be excluded as a suspect. In other instances, the investigator tried a sneak approach.

"I know you're nervous," Wolfe said over and over to witnesses waiting outside the grand jury room. "Would you like a drink of water before you go in there?"

The nervous men would usually drink the water and then return the cup, bearing a saliva sample, to Wolfe, who sealed it in a bag and shipped it off to the lab for analysis.

Others turned down the water, but accepted a slice of peppermint-flavored gum.

Wolfe was able to collect the used gum and saliva sample by advising that witnesses were not allowed to chew it in the courtroom.

Cigarette butts and inmate mail sent to county judges was also confiscated and sent for lab testing.

One inmate vehemently denied the women's request for his DNA, only to send them a letter further explaining why he refused. The envelope was sealed with his saliva.

The inmate was later ruled out, but the women found a little humor in the irony.

In one instance, Tanner and Wolfe drove to Lubbock to meet with the sister of a deceased witness so he could be excluded as a suspect.

When asked if she had any of her brother's belongings, the man's sister produced an old sports coat and the pair brightened upon seeing that the collar was stained, only to be disappointed.

"I wear it a lot," the woman said, hugging the coat. "It reminds me of my brother."

"Well, do you mind if we look in the pockets?" Tanner asked.

"No, that's fine," she said. "Help yourselves."

Wolfe, wearing gloves, reached into a side pocket and found a pink wedding napkin, folded and embossed with a couple's name and day of matrimony.

The napkin contained some dried mucus, also put through DNA testing.

"Hey," the woman said. "I remember that wedding."

"So, do you think your brother attended that wedding?" Tanner asked.

"Yes, he was there," she said.

The DPS crime lab was able to extract enough DNA from the napkin to create a sample, which excluded the man as a suspect.

In all, DNA from about 180 men was tested, but authorities were unable to find a match to the semen specimen.

The pool of possible suspects was so large and collection methods so varied, prosecutors scribbled their names on large dry erase boards and mounted them on the wall to keep track of them all.

Meanwhile, the public was growing impatient for justice. Tanner was certain that the grand jury proceedings would shake out new evidence, but the case wasn't moving along fast enough to satisfy the families.

It was 2003, a year after DNA linked Hartsfield and Pinkerton to the restaurant. Tanner believed she had enough evidence to indict Hartsfield, but the case was still riddled with problems.

Rangers Dowell and Elliott, whose testimony was critical to the investigation, were advancing in age and there was still a critical lack of documentation.

She sought out her old friend and mentor, Bill Turner, a respected criminal prosecutor, for fresh advice.

"Everyone in the world is all over my butt for not indicting them," Tanner said. "I'm at a loss here. What do I do?"

He answered with a question.

"Do you have any testimony from these guys?" he said.

"Did they lie?"

Tanner paused for a moment before answering.

"Yes."

"So why not indict for perjury?" he asked.

Tanner updated Dowell, one of her biggest skeptics, in private about plans to prosecute Hartsfield for lying under oath.

She knew the tough, towering Texan would be a hard nut to crack.

Dowell was a natural born lawman, serving in the Korean War before starting his law enforcement career as a patrolman in Corpus Christi and then working his way to being a Texas Ranger within the DPS.

Dowell appreciated the young attorney's tenacity, and she respected the hell out of him, both for the person he was and the expertise he had for working difficult, high profile cases, including interviewing serial killers Henry Lee Lucas and Otis Toole.

"Ranger, I need to update you on KFC," she said.

She told him about the DNA results, which put Hartsfield and Pinkerton at the restaurant, but as expected, the crusty lawman didn't act the least bit impressed.

"That DNA isn't nothin' but a bunch of Star Trek hocus pocus," he said. "Leave it out of the trial. Focus on the restaurant and the situation."

Tanner knew the Ranger was haunted by the KFC murders and she hoped the next bombshell she dropped might bring him a little peace, one day.

"We have DNA for a third suspect," she said, watching his eyes widen with interest.

Tanner told him about the discovery of the semen and the DNA identification of a third suspect, an African American.

Mankins, whom Dowell had pursued for years, is Caucasian.

The attorney detected a flicker of emotion from the lawman.

"Humph," Dowell said after a long pause. "Promise me something. Promise me you'll never give up on this case."

Chapter 18
Lawmen Question Delays

I n spite of the DNA breakthrough in the unsolved mass murder, years would pass with little or no movement to push the case to trial.

Tanner was aware of the public's frustrations, but she and others in the AG's office wanted to make sure the case, and its many twists and turns, was as complete as possible.

There would be no second chances to get it right.

There was good reason to be cautious. State officials had been wrong before and didn't want another black eye.

The public was still angry over the 1995 maneuver by the former Texas Attorney General to use the fingernail as a basis to indict Mankins for the murders, only to have the charges dropped after DNA tests did not link him to the crime scene.

Families, devastated by the repeated missteps, wanted justice and the opportunity to experience closure.

In spite of the revelation that there were new suspects linked by DNA, the case seemed to be going nowhere.

Rangers Elliott and Dowell, along with investigator Kieny, launched a rare maneuver, saying publicly in 2005 it was time for action.

Longtime investigators all liked and respected Tanner, but they could not understand her agency's hesitancy to take it to a jury.

The trio, in separate interviews, complained about the inaction, lamenting the fact they couldn't do more about it.

A frustrated Elliott, then 79, long revered for his calm demeanor under pressure, told the newspaper that time was not on his side.

In a sort of "tell all" to the reading public, the lawman said he felt it was a personal, negative reflection on him for the case to languish in file boxes collecting dust.

"It's discouraging and worries you," he said. "The people of Texas entrusted me with being a Texas Ranger and I wanted to produce. We had a lot of witnesses in the KFC case, but it just never came together."

He allowed the Tyler Morning Telegraph to conduct the interview at his home in Longview, Texas.

In that visit, he worried about dying before the case was solved.

"I've had this ever since the murders," he said, displaying an extensive case file filled with hundreds of pages of investigative notes and photographs.

"I went to different cities to track down leads, I went to prisons across the state, I talked to every drug dealer and user in the area, but no one would ever talk," he said.

Elliott said he knew from the moment he arrived that horrible Saturday morning in 1983, the case would be forever plagued with problems.

The restaurant crime scene had too many people trampling through it, but the murder site was in even worse shape.

"There were throngs of people gawking and walking around the bodies," he said, frowning at the recollection.

He shook his head in apparent disgust.

"It was chaotic, because there were people everywhere," he said. "The scene was basically contaminated from the start."

Elliott said he partnered with a Kilgore Police Department investigator before another Ranger arrived at the scene.

"We began collecting evidence and I'll never forget the

scene … it was unreal," he said. "I had worked multiple murders, but this one stood out above the rest."

Elliott said as days turned to weeks, investigators rounded up witnesses and assembled a growing list of suspects, but the evidence necessary to land a conviction was nowhere to be found.

"We never found the vehicle used to transport the victims or the other gun used in the murders," he said, admitting there was a discrepancy in some of the DNA evidence located inside the restaurant.

He didn't elaborate on what that evidence was, but the DNA collected inside the restaurant places several suspects at the scene; however, the chain of custody cannot connect the evidence to the person who collected it or submitted it for testing.

"I can testify that I saw it in the restaurant and that it came from there, but if we don't go to trial soon, then I won't be here to testify," he said.

Emotions bubbled to the surface when asked if he had any final remarks or regrets relating to the case.

"What do you mean, do I have regrets? Of course I do," he said, eyes flashing with anger. "I regret that we didn't get the evidence to finish this. I wanted to solve this so bad that I didn't let anything interfere with my work. It is solved, but we just never got everything we needed. If none of the suspects talk, then they will never be convicted and the case will remain open."

Dowell, about a year before his death, also shared his perspective on the old murder case from his home in Tyler.

Dowell retired in 1987 after serving more than 18 years with the Rangers.

He told the newspaper the KFC killings was the one case that would haunt him until the very end.

Aware of his own vulnerability amid declining health, the lawman, then 73, said he was fast becoming too fragile to testify. He worried about going to his grave with valuable testimony.

"This case was eating at me for a long time and I finally had to let it go," he said, shaking his head. "I still think about it when I see something in the news or one of the investigators on the case contacts me. I am ashamed and deeply disappointed in the system that has let these people suffer all these years without resolution - and it appears there will never be a resolution."

It seemed to be a significant statement, coming from a veteran lawman who had dealt with a lot of horrible things in his career.

The Ranger joined the investigation the day after the murders and served as custodian of some of the evidence. He attended the autopsies and helped console the families.

He was haunted by the brutality of the KFC murders and the helplessness of the innocent victims.

Dowell was a family man himself and felt the heavy weight of responsibility to help solve the case.

"I spent years chasing Jimmy," he said.

DNA proved him wrong, but even more frustrating was the state's delay in going after the very people state prosecutors believed committed the murders.

Dowell acknowledged the chain of custody on the box appeared somewhat weak at face value, but he believed the state had other evidence: one of the murder weapons.

Police investigators located a .38 caliber revolver they believe was used to execute the victims; the same weapon Mankins allegedly borrowed before the murders.

Authorities traced the gun back to the Houston Police Department, where it was used as a service revolver in the 1930s.

Little could be done to link it to the slayings because the barrel was damaged, Dowell said.

"The gun we recovered, when fired, left no distinguishing marks, because the barrel was damaged, but one of the guns used in the murders did the same thing," he said. "It was a leap for some to say it was the same gun."

The other weapon is believed to be a .357 Magnum revolver, which has yet to surface.

Dowell said the case was resolved, as far as he was concerned.

Two crimes were committed in the KFC case, he said, the

murders themselves and the lack of prosecution.

"We solved it," he said. "We just couldn't get anyone to do anything about it. I have never seen a more incompetent, flip-flop bunch of people as those at the AG's office. The DNA evidence is there to indict and why they are dragging their feet is beyond me. This case has gone on long enough."

Dowell died in May 2006, before the start of the capital murder cases. He was buried with full military honors in a quiet country cemetery in Whitehouse, Texas.

Former FBI agent Kieny, then 67, agreed with Dowell's assessment of the situation.

Kieny joined the FBI in 1969 and retired in 1995, but became involved with the investigation shortly after the murders.

"I've preached this fact for three years that we can't afford to wait any longer," he told the newspaper.

It wasn't until he became a Rusk County Sheriff's Office special investigator in 2001 under former Sheriff James Stroud that Kieny had total access to all the evidence.

What he found was shocking, even more perhaps than the crime itself.

"When I began finding all of the evidence, it was strewn between Dallas and Austin," he said. "It was preserved, but the fact was, that it was sitting in storage and no one was working the case. For seven years after the Mankins' indictment was overturned, the case sat idle. Why?"

Kieny and other investigators began entering DNA evidence into CODIS database to try and compare DNA from violent criminals and crime scenes from around the United States.

"In 2002, the case basically started from scratch again, because the CODIS system showed DNA collected at the scene matched several Texas Department of Criminal Justice inmates," Kieny said.

Those inmates were identified as Hartsfield, Pinkerton, Waters and two others: an inmate in Torres Unit in Medina and another in the Beto Unit in Tennessee Colony. Both inmates were questioned by authorities and cleared.

Hartsfield, Waters and Pinkerton all appear on the original suspect list obtained by the newspaper in the early days of the investigation.

Hartsfield's DNA was found inside the restaurant, near and around the kitchen - the scene of a fierce fight between the suspects and the victims.

Kieny said the grand jury met for months in 2004 to probe the case. Many jurors were disappointed when no capital murder indictments were handed up to the state.

"I was told the jurors wanted to indict, but the state did not," Kieny said, frowning.

The lawman said the breakdown in the chain of evidence, which Elliott and Dowell each discussed, was not enough to stall the case.

"We've already overcome some of that, but not all of it," he said, expressing concern over the passage of time. "If they (the prosecutors) don't hurry, then it won't matter, because there will be no one left to testify."

He said the state was uncooperative, repeatedly rejecting offers of assistance to set up a board of special prosecutors.

"I have this impression of the AG's office: They don't play well with others, meaning it's their game or no game," he said.

The public was aghast and demanded action.

The AG's office selected spokesman Jerry Strickland to try and defuse the criticism. His goal was to assure the public the KFC case was progressing and Attorney General Greg Abbott was staying informed on developments.

Strickland agreed the health and age of the lawmen closest to the investigation was a big concern for state prosecutors.

"We are working to preserve the testimony and evidence necessary to ultimately obtain convictions for capital murder," he said.

Authorities hoped Hartsfield's anticipated perjury trial would help capture some of the officers' testimony, before it was too late.

"We have no intention of the Hartsfield perjury indictment being the only indictment and charge coming out of the KFC case," Strickland said. "It is simply the only one pending at this time. Our investigation is ongoing and we are committed to the thorough investigation of the case."

103

Strickland would not address public speculation the state office was somehow unable to bring about resolution in the cold case.

"Our ultimate goal has been and always will be to obtain convictions of those responsible for capital murder," he said. "We will continue to work and speak with the families of those who died to make them aware of our progress."

Tanner read the lawmen's comments in the newspaper and felt the sting of the public thrashing.

She understood the frustrations, as well as the need to make sure the case was rock solid. She also cared about them and their opinions of her.

In her heart, she knew it was time to move forward.

"I understand why they are upset," she told Wolfe later. "We just need to make sure we are ready when the time comes to try those guys."

Chapter 19
Caught In a Lie

Micheal Jimerson, Rusk County's new district attorney, was still getting accustomed to the idea of his new role when word emerged that a prosecutor with the Texas Attorney General's Office wanted a meeting.

The new DA was a product of Rusk County, a hard-working farm boy whose parents insisted that education was critical for building financial stability. His mother was a teacher; his father, a cattleman with a keen sense for business.

Jimerson didn't grow up with aspirations of being a lawyer. He wanted to be an engineer, but found the coursework boring and tedious.

He adored government and history, opting instead for law school at Baylor University as a way to combine the subjects he found most interesting.

The young lawyer returned home after graduation, eager to try out his newfound knowledge and build a career.

But like so many others, he had to start off slow, working off court appointments before moving on to other specialty areas, including the "dust docket" for asbestos litigation.

Jimerson, part of six generations of a family born and raised in Rusk County, considered running for office only after strong nudging from certain community members, who wanted a change in the county political scene.

Kyle Freeman ran on a platform that centered largely on KFC, telling the community new developments in the case were just around the corner, while Jimerson focused more on court backlogs and other day-to-day judicial concerns.

Jimerson remembered being in middle school when five people were kidnapped from KFC and heard the stories about the discovery in the oil field. And as a product of Rusk County, he knew people related to the victims as well as the people involved in tracking down the killers.

In spite of their differing positions, both candidates agreed on one point as it related to KFC: the public needed closure.

If elected, Jimerson knew the community would expect his office to make meaningful progress in solving the cold case. He thought a lot of Freeman and hoped he was right about progress being made in the investigation.

It didn't take long after the 2004 win before Tanner came calling with the answers.

"I wanted to update you on where we are in the case," she said, offering an introductory handshake.

Jimerson listened as she ran through the case and was impressed the state was looking toward indictments.

"We have DNA on two people and we are continuing to look for the third," Tanner said. "When we find that third person, we can move forward."

The DA shook his head.

"No," he said. "You've got to go with what you have, the identity of the third person may surface along the way. This has hung over Rusk County long enough."

Jimerson acknowledged the need for caution, but argued that continued delays fed perceptions that law enforcement was somehow incapable of solving the crime.

"That's simply not the case," he said. "We've got to have some relief, we've got to get past this one."

"Okay," Tanner said. "But you are going to be right there

with me."

Television detectives seem to have the convenience of collecting copious amounts of evidence laden with DNA, but it was the just the opposite for Tanner's investigative team.

Authorities had Hartsfield's DNA at the scene, but little else linking him to the killings. No murder weapon, no fingerprints.

The clock was ticking.

Investigators who could attest to the chain of custody were growing frail and inpatient, calling out prosecutors to make their move.

Attorneys, embarrassed by the negative publicity, knew the lawmen were right - securing convictions in the case could be impossible without a record of their testimony.

The aging murder probe was fast becoming a situation of "now or never."

In the fall of 2005, Tanner and her team went after Hartsfield for lying to the special KFC grand jury charged with reviewing case evidence.

Grand jury proceedings are confidential, but the long-time suspect apparently told jurors he had never set foot inside the fast food restaurant even though Tanner had evidence proving otherwise.

Investigators searching the restaurant for evidence the night of the murders located a white box used for storing cash register tape splattered in blood. DNA tests conducted in 2001 showed the blood was a perfect match to Hartsfield.

As a result, Hartsfield, then 44, was facing a life sentence, not for killing the five people inside the KFC, but lying about it.

The bloody box was Tanner's key piece of evidence, but winning the opportunity to introduce it as such hinged on the credibility of retired Rangers Elliott and Dowell.

Elliott woke up early the day of the trial after a restless night of tossing and turning.

He didn't have much of an appetite, though he usually looked forward to breakfast.

On this morning, his mind was on more important things than food.

Elliott was no stranger to courtrooms, but this was no ordinary case in his career or anyone else who fought hard for its conclusion.

He, Dowell and others waited more than two decades to see the KFC killers brought to justice and his testimony this day would be a crucial step in resolving the case and giving the families some closure.

The retired Rangers arrived separately at the courthouse.

Elliott spotted his old counterpart, who was using a wheelchair for mobility.

"Stuart, how have you been?" he said, reaching for Dowell's hand. "Good to see you."

"You too, Glen," he said. "Glad to be here."

Inside the courtroom, Tanner and Wolfe, joined by Jimerson, spent a final few minutes assembling their case materials. There was a small mountain of paperwork associated with the case and they weren't afraid to show it off to jurors and court spectators.

"You'll do good," Wolfe said under her breath. "We're ready."

"Thanks," Tanner said. "I hope the jury sees it that way."

Defense attorney Joe Shumate was also ready. He knew the state might have a difficult time overcoming old investigative missteps and he planned to exploit the problems to the fullest extent of the law.

State District 4 Judge Clay Gossett, a fair, but stern judge, was hoping the trial would help soothe some of the unrest. He called the case to order.

Tanner, in her opening arguments, tried to ward off the damage, telling jurors the case had problems, but testimony from the original officers at the scene would place the evidence at the KFC and prove Hartsfield lied about never being there.

"A crime occurred that night that shook the foundation of this county," she said, facing the jury. "Finally technology caught up with the evidence. We want you to tell him, 'We know you were there that night.'"

Tanner called a parade of witnesses to help jurors visualize the enormity of the case. She addressed chain of custody concerns and investigative challenges up front.

Elliott testified he saw the bloody box when he arrived at the restaurant, but didn't collect it as evidence because he was summoned to the Rusk County oilfield to help investigate the discovery of five bodies.

Dowell said he couldn't specify which officer first collected the box as evidence, but he was the one who transported the box and other evidence to the Texas Department of Public Safety crime lab in Tyler for testing.

Former Tyler Police Department crime scene commander Doug Collard testified there wasn't much by way of fingerprints to work with at the time. He said the restaurant was a bad place to try and retrieve fingerprints because everything was coated in a layer of grease.

Pirtle, the Kilgore police detective, testified a lot of things went wrong in the case, starting with photographs taken of the crime scene. He said most of the film was ruined in development so there were few images recording the scene inside the restaurant.

The detective said it also took three weeks before a lead detective was named to head the investigation and by that time there was so much confusion, it was difficult to get anything done. Years into the investigation, no one could find the original evidence log.

Another witness reported seeing a white van in the KFC parking lot the night of the murders and remembered Hartsfield standing in line behind her to place an order.

The witness said she and other customers could hear one of the employees on the phone telling someone the night deposit had not been made and there was more than $2,000 in the restaurant.

Former restaurant manager Leanne Killingsworth confirmed about $2,000 was taken from the restaurant.

She said the deposit represented a "record day of business" and the restaurant should never have had that much money on hand, per company policy. The manager and assistant manager were required to make daily deposits and that didn't happen.

"I guess hindsight is 20-20," she said, crying. "We both got complacent in just making the deposit the next day."

After hearing from witnesses, Tanner tried to introduce jurors to the bloody box as evidence, prompting a series of objections from Shumate, who claimed there was no proof the box came from the eatery.

Gossett allowed the box to be introduced, despite a supposed break in the chain of evidence.

"Objection," Shumate persisted. "Your honor, we don't know where the box came from. There are no photographs of it being in the KFC, but somehow the box mysteriously appears in the possession of Stuart Dowell, who took it to the DPS crime lab in Tyler."

"Overruled," the judge said. "I'm going to allow it."

Lorna Beasley, DNA supervisor with the DPS crime lab in Garland, testified the blood found on the box belonged to Hartsfield and there was a one in 5.44 trillion chance, just in the African American community, the blood didn't belong to him.

Those odds increased when the DNA was compared to other races, she said.

Beasley also testified that the DNA found on the box was not that of former suspect Jimmy Earl Mankins Jr. or his former wife.

"That's all our witnesses, your honor," Tanner said, returning to her chair.

In a surprising turn of events, Shumate called his client to the stand.

Hartsfield insisted in taking the stand in his own defense, against the advice of counsel, Shumate said.

Tanner watched the defendant walk slowly to the witness stand and settle into the chair. He looked worried and a little nervous, chewing on his lip as he waited for the first question.

The prosecutor felt a wave of elation. This could be just the break she needed.

Shumate asked the man if he had ever visited the KFC in Kilgore.

"I have no recollection of ever being at that KFC," Hartsfield said. "I feel like I'm being framed."

Tanner saw an opportunity in cross-examination to discredit the testimony.

She highlighted Hartsfield's criminal history, which included the aggravated robbery of the Tyler convenience store, a drug conviction, engaging in organized crime and burglary.

There was also a reckless endangerment charge after he pointed a gun at a Tyler police officer in 1978, and witnesses who claimed to have seen him at the restaurant a few hours before the murders.

Tanner locked eyes with Hartsfield.

"So, I'm going to ask you again," she said. "Have you ever been to the KFC restaurant in Kilgore?"

"No."

Was it true he had a friend who owned a white van? And wasn't it true he borrowed the van from time to time?

"No," Hartsfield said. "That's not true."

The defendant's forehead began to glisten with sweat.

"Is it true you worked for an oil company shortly before the murders?" the prosecutor asked.

"That's true," Hartsfield said.

"No further questions," Tanner said, returning to her seat.

In closing arguments, the defense honed in again on the bloody box.

"The pressure is on investigators and prosecutors to do something in this case, but the box in question was only placed at the scene by Elliott," Shumate said. "It's their job to provide evidence and not ask you to fill in the gaps in their case. It is up to the state to prove where the box came from."

Shumate claimed the box "magically and mysteriously appeared" without any documentation from the crime scene.

Tanner fired back at the accusations, saying the evidence was covered in Hartsfield's blood, placing him inside the restaurant.

"He lied," she said, pointing at Hartsfield. "I am going to tell you to follow your oaths and if you follow them you will find him (Hartsfield) guilty. There is nothing magical about it as the defense claims. The technology finally caught up."

Jurors took a little more than two hours to find him guilty of aggravated perjury.

In the punishment phase, Tanner presented just one witness: Beverly Uzell, the former Tyler convenience store cashier, who faced Hartsfield from the wrong end of a gun on Sept. 26, 1983, two days after the KFC murders.

"He pointed a gun at me," she testified.

Shumate offered no witnesses and none of Hartsfield's family, some of whom attended the first several days of the trial, were present.

Hartsfield showed no emotion upon hearing his sentence: Life in prison.

Relatives of the five victims were seen weeping and hugging. This was not a capital murder conviction, but he would be behind bars nonetheless.

For Kieny, there was elation and satisfaction.

"I'm as happy as a lark," he said with a grin.

Tanner felt a wave of relief. She and Wolfe were making progress.

Perhaps the higher ups at the Attorney General's Office, the public and most important, the families of the victims, would be pleased.

"We still have a long way to go before this thing is over," Tanner told Wolfe later. "Now comes the hard part. Now we have to convict them of murdering those poor people."

Chapter 20
Facing a 'Monster'

In the fall of 2007, the quiet Bowie County Courthouse in New Boston seemed to transform overnight into a sea of spectators, lawmen and news media for the long awaited capital murder trial of one of the alleged perpetrators.

Romeo Pinkerton's trial, expected to take several weeks, was moved to the small town 120 miles northeast of Tyler due to decades of extensive media coverage.

Gossett agreed to the move knowing it would cost Rusk County taxpayers close to $1 million, but the KFC murder case was too well-known to be tried in East Texas.

Everyone knew about it and attorneys worried it could be difficult, if not impossible, to select a panel of unbiased jurors in Rusk County.

Gossett, Jimerson with several staff members, accompanied also by a bailiff, a court reporter and several District Clerk employees made the trip.

New Boston had become a temporary home to Tanner, Wolfe and a slew of others, but the question on everyone's mind was whether the case would result in a conviction.

The public was anxious for a conviction.

Hartsfield had been found guilty of aggravated perjury in 2005. Both men were indicted on capital murder charges after authorities said their DNA was linked to the crime scene.

Tanner was nervous about prosecuting the case. She hadn't slept well the night before and the soft scrambled eggs she tried to nibble at breakfast weren't sitting well, at all.

She watched as empty seats in the courtroom filled and studied the familiar faces in the crowd. They also seemed scared, foreheads twisted with worry.

"God, I hope this goes well," Tanner whispered to no one in particular.

At the next table, Pinkerton sat in silence, sometimes glancing behind him as if waiting on someone, but that someone never seemed to materialize. He appeared to be alone, except for his legal defense team.

Tanner wondered what thoughts were churning in his mind.

"All rise," the bailiff said as Judge Clay Gossett entered the chambers and took his place behind the bench. "You may be seated."

Fifteen jurors, eight women and seven men, settled into their chairs.

They looked like people who might live next door or down the street, mothers, dads and grandparents, all with serious expressions.

The judge read off a litany of guidelines and instructions before opening statements began. A gag order would discourage anyone from trying the case in the news media, lest they answer to the judge.

Tanner inhaled and stood up, preparing to drop a bombshell.

Looking each juror in the face, she first gave an overview of the case and why it was so complex to solve.

Five people were kidnapped from a Kilgore KFC and transported to a remote East Texas oil field where they were executed at close range.

The enormity of the mass murder scene swamped the resources of area law enforcement and the killers slipped through the dragnet of officers who responded to help solve the crime.

Decades passed. Witnesses died. Technology that could have helped solve the crime didn't exist at that time, she said.

Tanner said it took "fresh eyes" looking at the case in 2003 to see an obvious problem with the crime scene that had been overlooked.

"It was always assumed that Opie Hughes tried to run, but when new investigators began looking at the case, they began to see something else," the prosecutor said.

Seminal fluid was found in the crotch of her uniform pants, but the DNA profile created from that sample does not match any known individual, Tanner said.

"Even though the man has yet to be identified, the discovery of the semen is significant," Tanner said. "It means there was a third suspect present."

Audible gasps arose from the audience, capturing the attention of jurors.

Soft, silent tears began to trickle down the cheeks of some spectators.

Some simply sat motionless, stunned at the disclosure. Others clung to one another in search of comfort.

Tanner hated to surprise them like that, but she knew the information was too sensitive to share with anyone outside the tight inner circle of investigators.

"Despite Herculean efforts, to this day, there has been no DNA match made, but we know that there was a third person," she said. "This information was the closest-guarded secret in this entire case."

There was good reason for the secrecy, she said.

"This was by design to see if anyone knew there was a third person," she said. "The evidence was there all along ... the science just had to catch up."

Tanner tried to downplay the fact there were many missteps in the investigation by mentioning them at the start of the trial, before the defense had a chance to discredit the evidence.

One of the big errors was the pursuit of longtime suspect Jimmy Earl Mankins Jr.

Investigators had no real physical evidence linking him to the restaurant, only circumstantial evidence – a broken fingernail and his claims of knowing intimate details of the crime, the prosecutor said.

Cousins Pinkerton and Hartsfield were identified as possible suspects early on, but investigators were too eager to hang the murders on Mankins, a sort of small town outlaw with a lengthy rap sheet and an affection for street drugs.

So eager, it seemed, they ignored evidence that could have led them to the real killers, the prosecutor charged.

Ultimately the same science that would free Mankins from the noose of suspicion is what linked the crime to the two cousins, Hartsfield and Pinkerton.

Defense attorneys Jeff Haas and David Griffith anticipated Tanner's tactic, but they also had a game plan.

Griffith stood up and smoothed his dark-colored suit jacket. He knew they had to plant a seed of doubt in the minds of jurors in how the evidence was handled.

But Griffith knew better than to attack well-meaning lawmen, lest he anger the jurors, who might sympathize with their predicament. Instead, he would point out the obvious.

"In 1983, they had no knowledge of DNA because it didn't exist then," Griffith said.

Consequently, he added, investigators could not possibly know how to preserve it and protect it from contamination.

Griffith pointed out that while semen was detected on Hughes' work pants and blood stains found on Landers' clothing, neither sample is linked by DNA to Pinkerton and Hartsfield.

He urged the jurors to look past their emotions and concentrate on the cold, hard facts of the case.

"What I am asking the jury to do is follow the evidence," the defense attorney said. "This case is not only built on the evidence you hear, but also on the evidence you don't hear."

The state launched into its case against Pinkerton by starting at the beginning, summoning certain family members to testify about the events leading up to and following the murders.

Though years had passed, it was evident from the onset the wounds were still raw.

Billy Tyler was asked to describe his wife Mary's duties at the restaurant and the night he and stepdaughter, Kim, found the establishment in disarray.

"About 10:30, I called up there and didn't get any answer," he said. "At a quarter to 11, she still wasn't home, and I just had this feeling."

Tyler said he drove to the restaurant and saw no movement inside.

"There was trash next to the back door," he said. "The back door was open and that was unusual."

Hass, for the defense, asked Tyler to describe his stepdaughter's actions after they got inside.

"She opened the register up front and she said, 'The money is gone,'" he said, acknowledging during subsequent questioning of the teenager's troubled past and history of petty thefts.

Pirtle testified he was appointed lead detective about three weeks after the murders, but before that point, there was little semblance of order and coordination among those probing for clues.

"The detectives and all the agencies were going in their own directions," he said. "That made it more difficult to solve."

Pirtle recalled his initial role in the investigation, telling jurors he recovered two employee hats and a note to one of the male victims from a girlfriend.

He couldn't recall seeing a blood-smeared box or a crumpled paper napkin, crucial in the state's case against Pinkerton and Hartsfield, or who might have collected them.

Hartsfield's blood was said to be on both items, which became the centerpiece for his October 2007 aggravated perjury conviction and the cousins' capital murder indictments.

Former Kilgore Officer Wayne Reynolds, who later went to work as a trooper with the Texas Department of Public Safety, said he was sent to the restaurant to help search for the employees, but he didn't notice a bloody napkin.

"There were other paper-type products and things on the floor that would be in the restaurant, but I don't remember a specific one," he said. "I didn't make a notation of it in my report."

Haas asked about the integrity of the crime scene.

"You learned that other people had already been in the restaurant, correct?" Haas said. "Didn't family members of one of the victims go inside before police arrived?"

"Yes they had," Reynolds said.

Former KFC Manager LeAnn Killingsworth acknowledged under cross examination there had been a series of recent petty thefts happening within the restaurant.

"Weren't there significant problems with Kim and her mother?" Griffith asked.

She paused for a moment before answering.

There were problems, but I wouldn't say significant."

Griffith pressed on, asking about the Miller's reputed circle of "rough" friends.

"Wasn't her mother concerned?" he said.

Killingsworth said Mary Tyler was, indeed, concerned about her daughter's choice of friends, which did not seem to include the young outlaw, James Earl Mankins, Jr.

Ranger Elliott was also asked about the evidence.

He testified he was only in the restaurant about two hours before going to the oil field where the bodies were located, and that's probably why the box and napkin were not entered onto the evidence log.

"Did you keep any notes?"

"I'm not sure," he said. "I might have thrown them away. I can't be for certain."

The Ranger said he received a tip from then Smith County Sheriff Frank Brunt that Hartsfield, Pinkerton and a third man, Elton Winston, could be connected to the slayings so he made a "wanted for questioning" poster seeking information about their whereabouts.

Jurors also heard posthumous remarks from the late Texas Ranger Dowell, who testified during Hartsfield's 2005 aggravated perjury trial.

The defense fought to suppress the remarks because they would be unable to cross-examine him.

"I'll allow it," the judge said. "The jury should be allowed to hear it."

In other testimony, Wolfe, as investigator for the Texas Attorney General's Office, said she found it curious that Hughes' underwear was missing.

It didn't seem reasonable that a devoted wife and mother would forgo underwear in a hot, scratchy polyester work uniform - coupled with the fact that there was no explanation as to why her body was found so far away from the others, she said.

"I had my suspicions," she said.

Without proof the theory was a best guess, so she had to go hunting for something more concrete.

She recalled asking Tyler Police to examine the slacks and see if anything showed up when the pair of uniform slacks was put under a laser.

"There was a large stain in the crotch area," she told the jury.

Forensic investigators working at the DPS lab in Garland said the stain was semen, but the DNA could not be matched to a known person, even when compared to samples maintained in state and national databases.

State's witness Lorna Beasley, who served as DNA lab supervisor for the DPS lab in Garland, said she attended the Sept. 1, 2001 meeting with the Attorney General's Office to examine various items of the victims' clothing that were never tested by DPS.

A decision was made to test the clothing as well as retest the napkin, held previously by another lab during the case involving Jimmy Mankins Jr.

The DNA did not match any of the victims or Mankins.

Beasley testified when they tested the clothing, a blood stain on Landers' shirt did not belong to the victim and there has never been a match to any known person.

Tanner opened several paper bags containing the victims' clothing so jurors could see the items being discussed.

In many respects, it was like a time capsule.

There was Mary Tyler's blue-green pullover blouse and jeans; Opie Hughes' brown work uniform with her comfortable red and white athletic shoes.

Jurors saw also traces of individual personalities: Joey Johnson's black net pullover and blue jeans; Monte Landers' black vest and red/blue striped pullover; David Maxwell's gray coveralls and white "Foot Joy" athletic shoes.

Beasley testified the shirt triggered curiosity about some old evidence from the 1983 KFC murders that was still stored in the lab.

She and her boss, Manuel Valadez, found the possibilities so intriguing, they decided it might be worth a second look, in case advances in science turned up something new.

Back in 1983, there were limited tests for blood - scientists could hone in on different types, but little else.

But with the advent of DNA testing, it was possible to learn much more about a person's blood.

"Each person, unless they are identical twins, has unique characteristics, even among blood relatives," she said.

Beasley said she was able to obtain a complete DNA profile from blood splattered on a box from the restaurant, but the real break happened in October 2001 when the national CODIS, short for Combined DNA Indexing System, database came up with a match.

It belonged to Pinkerton's cousin, Darnell Hartsfield.

Several jurors leaned forward, riveted by the testimony.

Tests on another key piece of evidence – a bloody napkin – pinpointed the identity of another known individual: Romeo Pinkerton.

Authorities obtained DNA samples from the men for comparison and the results confirmed the findings.

"What are the chances it could belong to someone else," Tanner asked.

Extremely slim, Beasley said, adding, "About 1 in 942.2 trillion."

"Objection," Griffith said, complaining the numbers were speculative at best.

"I'll allow it," the judge said. "The science is well-documented."

The defense started pounding on lab procedures and the possibility of contamination.

But Beasley stood her ground, saying the items tested had been safely stored and preserved in the lab since 1983.

Kieny, the former FBI agent, also testified, saying he and a Texas Ranger collected blood samples and a statement from Pinkerton, who denied playing a role in any robberies or burglaries with his cousin.

"Would you please read his statement into the record?" Tanner asked.

Kieny read the following excerpt:

"I was accused and questioned about the murders of the people in Kilgore, Texas and I was cleared when the police backtracked where I was at the time of the KFC murders. I told the police I was in prison at the time of the murders ... I have never been to the KFC restaurant in Kilgore and couldn't even tell you where it was at."

Kieny said Pinkerton offered no explanation when advised DNA matched his blood to a sample found in the restaurant.

He said Pinkerton denied visiting the restaurant and claimed the blood found inside did not belong to him.

There were other instances in which the suspect fudged the facts.

Kieny said that contrary to Pinkerton's claims his release from prison was delayed due to complications from Hurricane Alisha, he had records showing the inmate was released two days prior before the murders.

Under cross examination, Kieny acknowledged the case had been frustrating.

He also denied seeing photos or notations documenting the presence of the box and napkin.

Haas also hinted that Pinkerton's signature on his statement seemed similar to Kieny's. The attorney said it would have been helpful if Kieny had made a tape recording of the visit, lest questions arise along the way.

"I guess you'll have to take my word for it," the lawman said.

Prosecutors produced earlier documents featuring Pinkerton's signature and the style appeared to remain similar.

Haas also questioned him about a white van, believed similar to one seen leaving the crime scene. The van, previously owned by Robert Franklin, a friend of Winston.

Franklin, who also testified, said he moved to Tyler in the early 1970s after accepting a scholarship to play basketball for Texas College and Winston moved with him

Franklin said he started his own cleaning service, relying on a windowless 1970s model white Ford van for a work vehicle.

The witness said he loaned his work van to Winston on several occasions and through his friend met Hartsfield, but he couldn't recall ever meeting Pinkerton.

Franklin said he didn't own the van the state admitted into evidence - the vehicle needed some expensive repair work so he sold it for $50 to a man who thought he could fix it.

Former Tyler Police Officer Mike McCarty said he stopped a speeding white van around 2:30 a.m. in the northern area of the city in March 1984. The driver was Elton Winston and the vehicle was a 1974 Ford van. Winston was taken into custody for driving with a suspended license.

Witness Samuel Johnson said he was traveling on Texas Highway 135 in Kilgore about a week after the murders when he avoided colliding with a large white van that had run a stop sign.

The driver responded to the incident with "hand gestures," he testified.

Johnson said he was later contacted by law enforcement who asked him to look at a photo lineup to see if he recognized anyone. He identified the driver as being one of the men featured on an old flyer that contained photos of Pinkerton, Hartsfield and Winston.

The poster was a copy of the one Ranger Elliott created after the murders.

Inmate Ronald Null said he has been incarcerated in federal prison in Seagoville for facilitating a cell phone in the commission of a felony, but it was while he was housed in the Smith County Jail he met Romeo Pinkerton.

Null said that while spending time in a holding cell, he reviewed Pinkerton's case file, which outlined key components of the investigation and the significance of the bloody napkin.

He thought it was odd that Pinkerton asked if DNA could still be on that napkin.

"Trying to keep it light," I told him, "Look you're not O.J., so if that's your blood, then it will still be there," Null told the jury. "I told him if he could put himself hundreds of miles away from there, that's what he should do."

Null told Assistant State Prosecutor Laura Popps that

Pinkerton confided that he lied to authorities, telling them he was stuck during bad weather in the Houston area at the time of the murders when in fact, he was in Tyler.

Griffin countered the claims, pressing Null to divulge the rest of the story.

"Isn't it true that he (Pinkerton) never told you he did anything in the KFC case," the attorney asked. "And he felt he was being brought into the case because he and his cousin Darnell Hartsfield ran around together?

"That's correct," Null said, nodding in agreement.

Griffith continued.

"And didn't he tell you that the robbery was his cousin's style and not his, and that he didn't like confrontations. Right?"

Again, Null agreed.

Griffith wrapped up his cross examination, asking point blank if Pinkerton ever admitted to being at the restaurant.

Null said Pinkerton did not put himself at KFC, but he did describe his role in other unrelated robberies carried out with his cousin.

The state asked Null if he expected any deal for his testimony.

"No," he said. "I'm getting out in May – I've done my time."

A pivotal moment in testimony came from a former Smith County Jail inmate turned state's witness, who said Pinkerton seemed to know details about the slayings others might not.

The witness said he spent about eight months in jail awaiting transfer to another facility after pleading guilty to drug charges. During his stay, he met Pinkerton, who was about to be tried for capital murder.

"He seemed quiet and laid back," the witness said. "We started playing chess together."

When another cellmate pointed out Pinkerton's picture in the newspaper, the witness said the publicity was Pinkerton's business and no one should be discussing it.

Pinkerton later brought up the subject on his own.

"What happened?" Tanner asked.

"We were playing chess, and he brings this murder thing up

from the article and asked what I knew about it," the witness said. "I didn't know about it and basically didn't want to know about it."

The witness said he asked Pinkerton the same question and received a chilling response: Pretending to pull the trigger of an imaginary handgun.

The witness said he reported the gesture to his defense attorney, who updated Tanner and Wolfe.

He also agreed to be outfitted with a small microphone in hopes of capturing additional conversations, but those were largely drowned out by background noise.

The gun gesture left a lasting impression.

"You can tell when someone is making something up and when they aren't, and that look in Romeo's eyes, I will never forget it," the witness said.

Tanner listened intently.

She felt good about the progress of the trial, now in its second week, and wondered what twists the defense might be planning.

This whole thing could have been avoided, if Pinkerton would only admit to his role in the slayings.

And then it happened, a window of opportunity during a break.

"They want to talk," Tanner told her assistant prosecutor. "Do you think?"

Popps, the assistant prosecutor, was looking smug. "Maybe."

Gossett ended Friday testimony by announcing a recess until Tuesday.

As the spectators prepared to leave, relatives of the victims were ushered into an adjoining room for a closed door meeting.

They emerged about an hour later, tight-lipped and tense.

A few days later, as jurors made their way back into the courtroom after a weekend off, Gossett welcomed them with a few words of praise.

"We all appreciate the sacrifices that you have given," he said, acknowledging the difficulties of being separated from family.

Several jurors nodded in appreciation of the remarks and glanced at Pinkerton, who was looking down at his hands.

An eerie hush fell over the courtroom as Gossett continued.

"We've had some developments," he said.

Attorneys worked up a plea agreement. Pinkerton agreed to plead guilty to five counts of murder and received five life sentences.

"We needed to keep this information from you, in the event he changed his mind," the judge said.

Entering a plea of guilt spared him from the death penalty, but it also meant the remainder of his days would likely be spent behind steel bars and concrete walls.

He would eventually be considered for parole, but his criminal past would probably keep him from walking free again.

The agreement did not require him to divulge details of the crime, a practice known as allocution. Prosecutors said they had no leverage to force the suspects to talk.

Gossett said the families, having been updated earlier, agreed to the terms of the agreement. The update also allowed them the opportunity to decide whether to speak to the defendant and jot down a few notes.

"To the jurors, your jobs are not quite over," Gossett said. "You must follow strict instructions to not discuss your opinions on guilt or innocence while the case against his cousin is still pending."

Families of the victims took turns addressing Pinkerton face to face, but there was no hiding the weight of their anguish.

One of the first to speak was Opie Hughes' daughter, Myra.

"Part of my life died with her," she said, reading from a sheet of note paper.

Myra Hughes was 16 when her mother was murdered, during those awkward teenage years when mother-daughter relationships are so important.

She had the support of a loving father, but the enormity of her mother's absence affected her entire life as well as that of her family.

Their last conversation had been an argument, but she felt fortunate it ended with Opie Hughes telling her daughter she loved her, Myra Hughes said, choking back emotion.

It was the last time she would hear her mother utter those three precious words or feel her warm embrace.

Myra and her little brother, Merle, who was just 11 when his mother was murdered, grew up longing to see her mother's dimpled smile and smell the rich goodness of her home cooked meals.

There were no more of her good night kisses.

While friends and classmates were laughing and teasing with parents at bedtime, they grew up dreading the darkness and heaving sobs of despair that seemed to accompany it.

There was no closure to the heartache or innocence lost.

"I cannot begin to emphasize my sadness and anger," Myra Hughes said, facing her mother's killer.

Merle Hughes, now a grown man, said from the time his mom died, his young world was turned upside down.

"I wanted to be with my friends, but I didn't want to leave my father alone because I was afraid of what would happen to him," he said.

Pinkerton turned away when a furious Jack Hughes began speaking of his late wife.

Hughes struggled for years to fill the void left by his wife, trying at the same time to be father and mother to his devastated children.

"Look at me," he shouted. "You had no right. No one has the right to be the animal that you are."

He paused, waiting for the convicted man to look him in the eyes.

"Thank you for looking at me," Hughes said, taking a deep breath for composure. "I want you to think of me for the next 100 years. When you draw your last breath of life, that's when your punishment will begin."

Linda Landers was fighting to contain her emotions before she said a word about her precious son, Monte, the skinny-armed, funny 19-year-old with a contagious laugh.

Between sobs, she told Pinkerton about trying to survive the first night after learning of his death.

"I just remember screaming," she said, describing the unimaginable pain that never seemed to ease.

The courtroom was quiet, except for occasional sniffles

from spectators and jurors.

For months after his death, Linda Landers said she tried to shelter her four other children from the hurt Pinkerton caused.

About a year after his killing, she realized that she did not die with her son and she must be strong for the other children left behind.

It was difficult, but she learned to cope with the emotional emptiness to help her family.

Looking squarely at Pinkerton, the anguished woman said the pain left by the murder will never heal.

"There isn't a day that goes by I don't remember that laugh, that little curl of hair he had on his head when he was a baby," she said, her face streaked with tears. "My heart is pulled out by the roots."

The convicted man showed no reaction.

He sat there, staring, as if he could see right through her, as courtroom spectators passed around tissues to dab their eyes.

When Kathy Hamilton took the stand to talk about her brother, David Maxwell, she spoke of the difficult years that followed his death.

"Our family fell apart from the stress," she said.

Her father's health declined, the family business fell into bankruptcy. Years later, her other brother committed suicide, she said.

Pinkerton sat motionless, looking the other way.

"Please, look at me," she said, her voice rising in anger. "You are not only a murderer, but a coward."

Maxwell's wife, Lana Maxwell Dunkerley, took the stand and spoke in a tiny, childlike voice that more closely resembled that of an 18-year-old girl, her age at the time of her husband's death, rather than the woman in the witness stand.

She described herself as a chubby girl who may not have turned everyone's head, but David, a playful college fraternity member, saw past her insecurities and married her.

She was pregnant with their first child when David died, she said, eyes fixed on Pinkerton.

"When you're 18 years old and you get married, you don't think bad things will happen," she said. "It wasn't until I reached in that casket and felt his hand I knew that was my

David."

She studied the convict's face, searching for some sign, any sign, he was listening, but Pinkerton stared straight ahead.

"I don't think you're really sorry for what you did, and there isn't any way for me to shame you into it," she said.

Her son David Maxwell, Jr., then 23, followed up his mother's remarks, saying Pinkerton robbed him of a lifetime of memories.

He grew up to become a successful businessman, but his life never felt complete.

Other families got to enjoy their loved ones before they died, but Maxwell – who inherited his father's expressive eyes and easy-going grin - said he will never know his father or the kind of man he was, all because of a press of a trigger.

"I have nothing," he said. "All I have are the stories people tell me and the photos they show me. You were facing the death penalty, and you got to say no. You can't stand up and take your punishment like a man. You should be ashamed of yourself for wimping out."

Also taking the stand was victim Mary Tyler's daughter, Kimberly Miller.

She described the hatred in her heart, her stare fixed on Pinkerton.

Her hands trembled as she read from a pre-written statement, "I hope you miss everyone you ever loved, if you ever loved anyone."

A relative of Joey Johnson described the teenager as someone who loved life, people and church, but her memories of him are forever tainted.

"I never thought this day would come and I would get to confront the monster of my dreams," she said. "I can't think of him without thinking of you, and I don't want to think of you. You make me sick."

At no time during the testimony of the surviving family members did Pinkerton display a hint of remorse.

The judge remanded Pinkerton to state custody.

He rose from the defendant's chair and walked calmly out of the courtroom in shackles, flanked by sheriff's deputies.

Family members dabbed their eyes and sniffled, troubled at

the cool demeanor displayed by the man who had just pleaded guilty to gunning down their loved ones.

Gossett, from the bench, was more compassionate in his thoughts. "May God be with each of you."

Tanner sat alone with her thoughts late that night, wondering if Pinkerton's decision to plead guilty would bring about any real healing for the families. She felt some relief at having wrapped up the trial, but her mood was somewhat melancholy.

The sudden ring of her cell phone startled her.

"Feel better?" Wolfe's voice asked.

"Sorta. You?"

"Same," Wolfe said. "It's not over."

"Nope," Tanner said. "One down, more to go."

Chapter 21
Hartsfield on Trial

T anner and Jimerson were ready in the fall of 2008 when it was Hartsfield's time to face the jury. They felt confi-i dent from the last go-around that the pieces were there to put the second of two cousins behind bars.

It was just a matter of putting them together.

They had DNA putting Hartsfield at the scene of the murders, numerous experts and the momentum of Pinkerton's conviction to help support the case.

Another change of venue was granted to ensure the defendants received fair trials, which called for moving the proceedings from East Texas to Bryan-College Station, home of the Aggies.

Eight women and six men, including a College Station police officer, were selected to serve as jurors with two alternates.

The courtroom was sleek and modern down to the last detail, outfitted with the latest technology and finishes, a stark contrast for trying a murder case within days of its 25th anniversary.

Prosecutors were feeling the heat.

"I think we're ready," Tanner whispered, watching court bailiffs escort Hartsfield to his seat at the defense table. "I think they know it too."

Jimerson grinned and nodded in agreement.

Hartsfield, seated nearby, looked uneasy and tried not to think about the burning stares coming from some audience members. His sister was also in the audience, and Hartsfield seemed to be both comforted and saddened by her presence.

Defense attorneys Don Killingsworth and Thad Davidson huddled together, reviewing several pages of notes before the proceedings got under way.

The men seemed confident they could shoot holes in the state's case and they whispered to the defendant, passing on information and encouragement.

Davidson, in his opening remarks, began attacking the integrity of the investigation. He honed in on what was portrayed as flimsy evidence collection and the mystery surrounding a cash register receipt box, which DNA experts said tested positive for having Hartsfield's blood on it.

He said DNA should not be the sole factor in determining his client's guilt or innocence.

"DNA is not a magic Band Aid," Davidson said. "It does not cure gaping wounds in a case."

Tanner opened by telling jurors their job was to consider the facts and help bring closure to a case for the victims and their families.

Tanner admitted there were obstacles, but she was confident the evidence would lead to a conviction.

Hartsfield faced multiple life sentences. The state removed the death penalty from the case, sparing Hartsfield the possibility of living the remainder of his days on Texas' death row.

Hartsfield was relieved he would not face the needle, although he didn't relish the thought of living out his days in a concrete cage either.

He'd heard plentiful stories that sometimes the lethal injections didn't work as intended and inmates died a slow, horrible death, fighting for air, unable to move or cry out in pain as the toxic brew passed through their bodies.

Hartsfield looked uncomfortable when Maxwell's former wife, seated in the witness stand, told jurors it was hell to be 18-years-old and a widow.

Lana Maxwell Dunkerley said her husband never got a chance to meet his only child, and she struggled throughout his upbringing to be both a mother and father to him.

Jurors also heard accounts from Jack Hughes, testifying about the loss of his wife, Opie, and Mary Tyler's husband, Billy Tyler, who spoke of finding an empty restaurant and the fear of not knowing what happened to her.

Tyler was also questioned about his stepdaughter's troubled background.

Killingsworth asked if it was true Kim was stealing from the KFC.

"No, she wasn't stealing from the restaurant," Tyler said. "She did take things from me and my wife."

"Is it true she did it even after your wife's death?"

"Yes," Tyler said. "She did."

Brown, the investigator, testified he worked the crime scene from midmorning the day the bodies were found until late afternoon when evidence was taken to the Rusk County Jail.

Davidson asked if he was aware of any fingerprints or blood connecting Hartsfield to the oil field scene.

"No I am not."

On a redirect from Tanner, Brown said no DNA or finger-prints, other those belonging to the victims, were found at that location.

Jurors also heard from Reynolds, the first officer responding to the restaurant that night.

He testified he never saw a box at the restaurant, but he wasn't looking for evidence either. His primary purpose in being there was to search for victims or suspects who might still be inside, so he did not stop to collect or photograph evidence.

Former KFC manager Leann Killingsworth, no relation to counsel, said after receiving word "something wasn't right at the restaurant," recalled having a bad feeling.

She testified several money bags were found to be missing,

along with the day's receipts. It appeared no one had time to finish their work for the evening because the time cards showed the employees never clocked out.

Leann Killingsworth said she learned about the deaths from her cousin, who was a police officer.

And though decades had passed, the trauma of the experience was still raw. She cried while recalling the trip to Dallas to identify the bodies of the victims.

"I wanted to do it for the families," she said, wiping her eyes. "I didn't want them to have to do it."

As testimony continued, the defense spent the first week hammering away at obvious flaws in the investigation, starting with the disappearance of the Kilgore Police Department's evidence log.

The log, viewed as critically important to document the chain of custody, detailed the collection and whereabouts of key pieces of information about the case, seemed to vanish into thin air.

Pirtle said the evidence log was there when he was working for the department. Sometime after he left the department, it disappeared.

He could not recall seeing a blood-covered box or a napkin in the restaurant during his initial visit to the crime scene.

"So when did you become aware of the bloody box and napkin?" Killingsworth, the attorney, asked.

"It was during a meeting about three or four days later," he said, explaining agencies involved in the case did not share information on a regular basis.

Consequently, if someone submitted case evidence without reporting it to the other agencies, it wasn't easy to find out about it.

The state called witness Lynetta Ashley, a former KFC employee who earned the macabre nickname "Lucky Lynetta" because she didn't have to stay late and close for the evening. Her mother picked her up before the robbery and murders.

Ashley could not recall if there was a box stored under the counter that night.

"There should have been," she said. "There was no reason to remove the box, but that was years ago, so I would have to say no."

Davidson asked if she remembered any black men being in the KFC the night of the murders.

"I don't remember, but I am not going to say there wasn't," she said.

Davidson pressed on, asking if she observed any other vehicles in the parking lot when she left that evening.

"No, I did not."

Tanner redirected the question, asking where she usually parked.

Ashley said her mother picked her up in front of the restaurant, not in the rear, so she would not be able to see if a vehicle was parked in back.

In other witness testimony, former Tyler police officer Doug Collard said that Kilgore police called his crime scene unit to the KFC to process the evidence at the restaurant.

The first thing he noticed pulling into the parking lot was the news media standing too close to the crime scene. He asked that barricades be erected around the parking lot and the media moved further away.

Collard said there was so much foot traffic inside the restaurant, evidence that might have been discovered was forever lost amid a jumbled mess of footprints.

Tanner asked if some of the evidence could have been collected prior to his arrival.

"I was told later that was the case," he said frowning in apparent frustration.

Tanner pointed out that removing evidence before the scene is documented is problematic because it alters the scene. Crime scenes are typically photographed from multiple angles to document the environment and the items in it.

"Is that common for multiple agencies to be involved with evidence collection process?" Tanner asked.

"No," he said. "If they were going to do it, there was no reason to call us."

Collard said some police departments in those days were unaccustomed to large crime scenes and did not have a protocol for handling them.

During his time in the restaurant, Collard said he took photos of a stain on a lower shelf under the cash register and in proximity of a large pool of blood on the floor.

He didn't recall seeing a bloody box or napkin, but said it was possible another officer collected the evidence and presented it to the DPS crime lab.

The judge later announced a short recess, giving Tanner an opportunity to prepare for the fireworks.

She planned to introduce testimony given in 2005 by the late Ranger Dowell, who died the following year.

The Ranger spent years trying to link Mankins to the murders, believing the suspect's torn fingernail was a match to the one recovered from Johnson's clothing.

Tanner worked hard to convince the veteran lawman that DNA was the best way to convict the culprits, but Ranger Dowell could never accept the idea technology was a better crime fighter than experience.

Nonetheless, he was pleased to testify in Hartsfield's earlier aggravated perjury trial, clarifying the origins of the box to complete the chain of custody.

Tanner knew Ranger Dowell was afraid his declining health would win out and he would not live long enough to see justice for the families.

Dowell was dependent on a wheelchair when he took the stand in 2005 to testify that he was the one who received a blood splattered box from former Kilgore Police Capt. Marvin Avance, who removed both the box and a bloody napkin from inside the KFC before other detectives arrived. Avance was in poor health at that time and unable to testify.

Tanner was anxious to read his testimony into the record, knowing the defense would put up a fight.

"Ladies and gentleman, I would like to read the testimony of Ranger Stuart Dowell," she said.

"Your honor, this is unfair," Davidson said, saying there was no opportunity for cross examination and the state didn't list him as a witness.

Tanner fired back, telling the court there was already a basis to use testimony from another proceeding, so this jury should be allowed to hear it too.

"It would be silly to put a dead person on the witness list," she said. "He is not on any witness list."

The prosecutor said although the perjury trial was a different proceeding, it was interlaced with the capital murders - Hartsfield had been inside the KFC restaurant, but told the grand jury he had never been there.

Davidson wasn't buying it.

"Lying to a grand jury about being in a KFC is not the same as killing five people in another county," he argued.

Gossett said he would consider the matter and announce his decision at a later time.

As the first week of testimony drew to a close, Tanner was looking forward to a mental break, albeit a brief one. There was plenty to review before trial resumed.

This was the second capital murder trial in about a year for Tanner and Jimerson and the stress was grueling for all involved.

"How do you think it is going?" she asked Jimerson.

"I feel pretty good about it," he said. "As you know, there's no such thing as a perfect case, but you've done your homework."

The judge later agreed with the state, ruling Dowell's earlier testimony was admissible.

Tanner breathed a sigh of relief. Gossett's decision was a good way to start the second week of testimony, which coincided with the 25th anniversary of the slayings.

She knew, as did the defense, Dowell's testimony was critical for establishing a credible chain of custody for the box, which became suspect after the evidence log disappeared and film from the crime scene was ruined during development.

Jimerson read Dowell's testimony into record, telling jurors at the time he collected the white box from Avance, the police officer was acting as the custodian of evidence.

Dowell said he transported the box to the Department of Public Safety lab after the murders.

Ranger Elliott was next to testify, explaining he and Kilgore detective Danny Pirtle started taking photos of evidence at KFC, but were called away from the scene after the bodies were found.

Davidson pressed Elliott about the blood spatter he observed in the restaurant.

The defense attorney produced three white boxes with his own blood on them in an attempt to trick Elliott, asking if he saw any differences between the three boxes in his possession and the one allegedly found in the restaurant.

Elliott, a blood spatter expert, pointed out the differences.

"One is a castoff," he said. "The others had blood dabbed onto the boxes and not the same type of pattern as the box taken from KFC."

Elliott acknowledged both the restaurant and oil field where the bodies were found were not handled properly and may have been contaminated, but he stood firm on the origins of the evidence.

Glen Johnson, a former DPS firearms examiner in Tyler, was also called to testify. He said several of the bullets fired during the KFC murders showed at least two different firearms were used.

"We had many firearms submitted to us over the years," he said, responding to questions. "I probably test fired over 50 Smith and Wesson firearms. There were many more that were brought into the laboratory that I didn't accept because the characteristics did not match any of the evidence bullets."

Johnson said there was never a gun submitted that matched the markings of any of the 11 bullets recovered in the case.

Davidson asked about the possibility that a gun linked to James Earl Mankins Jr. had been altered.

"There were no indications that there were obvious alterations to the barrel of that weapon," Johnson said. "You can tell that by looking at it, by holding it up to the light."

Davidson asked if the gun was the same one used in the crime.

"I could not eliminate it," Johnson said. "It's possible, but I did not see any evidence."

John Beene, DPS forensic scientist, was a chemist in 1983 and logged several pieces of evidence in the KFC case in Tyler.

Beene testified he accepted a white box with Type O blood on it, a bloody napkin and plastic cup from Dowell and sent it to Garland. The items were sent via mail plane on Oct. 4, 1983.

When questioned by the defense as to why the "official

139

submission form" did not have a case number on it, Beene answered, "We all knew what case it was and not every piece of paper had one on it."

Jurors also heard from Lorna Beasley, the DPS scientist who testified in Pinkerton's trial, about the decision to retest items still in storage at the lab.

She told jurors she was in the Sept. 11, 2001 meeting at the Texas Attorney General's office when it was decided to retest certain items.

The meeting took place, even as the nation was under attack by terrorists. The team watched the events unfold on TV, but everyone refocused on the case before them.

The bloody napkin had been taken to a private lab years earlier for DNA testing, but Kieny resubmitted it to the DPS lab the day after the meeting.

Beasley said the DNA profile did not match the DNA profile on the box, which meant there was blood from two unknown individuals in the restaurant.

Scientists submitted the DNA profile on the box to CODIS in July 2001 followed by the napkin in December 2001.

"Did anything significant happen after the DNA profiles were submitted? Tanner asked.

"Yes."

On Oct. 22, 2001, Beasley testified she received notification there was a possible match on the box. An affidavit was issued to her and the investigating officer in the case to obtain DNA from the possible match. The database identified Darnell Hartsfield as being a match.

Beasley said notification came from CODIS on Jan 8, 2002, naming Romeo Pinkerton, Hartsfield's cousin.

Both men's names appeared on the initial suspect list created after the murders.

Beasley also testified that semen taken from Hughes' pants has not been matched to anyone in the data or anyone who has provided a sample.

Her boss, Manuel Valadez, said the box the state offered into evidence was the same box tested by the lab.

"How can you be so sure?" Tanner asked.

"Well," he said. "Barely visible are my initials and case

number and also I remember the box, because it's kind of hard to forget a case that has five victims."

In other testimony, Robert Giles, Orchard-Cellmark director of operations, said he conducted DNA testing on the fingernail found in Johnson's clothing and compared it to samples from Mankins and then later samples of the bloody napkin.

Giles told jurors that the DNA typing his company did on the fingernail was inconclusive, but noted later tests showed the fingernail was not Mankins, even though he was found to be missing a nail from the same finger after the murders.

Killingsworth, who died in December 2011, asked if Giles could say for certain, based on the testing his company conducted, the nail did not belong to Mankins.

Giles was vague in his response.

He said that based on the results, there could be two people in the courtroom that are the same typing.

Scrutiny over advances in the science continued with Dr. Herbert McDonald testifying in a video deposition that a fingernail presented to him was not a match to Mankins.

"There is absolutely no comparison between them," McDonald said.

Forensic scientist Rhonda Roby, a world-renowned expert in DNA, agreed.

She told jurors she worked for the Armed Forces Institute of Pathology when the lab was asked to perform DNA testing on the fingernail presumed to be Mankins.

Roby said the lab agreed to conduct the tests after former Texas Sen. Phil Gramm sent a letter to the secretary of the Army, asking for assistance.

It was the first time the institute performed DNA testing on nails, so they first conducted a study using samples of their fingernails and blood to determine the best way to extract DNA.

Their tests even included a nail sample that was several years old and scientists discovered it was possible to test the material and receive consistent results.

An unexpected finding emerged when the lab tested the assumed Mankins' nail.

"That fingernail fragment could not have come from James

Mankins or a maternal relative of his," Roby said. "The DNA found in the fingernail matched the DNA found in Mary Tyler's known fingernails clipped during autopsy."

But lawmen investigating the KFC killings weren't so quick to buy into the findings, Roby said, adding, "They were reluctant to accept the fingernail did not come from Mr. Mankins."

Davidson, under cross examination, asked Roby if she knew the origins of the fingernail or if anyone was concerned it could have been switched with another sample.

"I wouldn't say we believed it was switched," she said. "I think we heard, and were informed of concerns from the attorney general's office about the fingernail. We never had fear about what we had received."

The scientists, responding to other inquiries, said DNA could be damaged by certain substances, and degrade over time, but not change.

"DNA is DNA," Roby said. "If I get one result it is not going to flip over to another type because of degradation or inhibitions. It is still going to be the same DNA."

Kieny also took the stand, testifying he not only worked the case as a federal agent, but was hired by former Rusk County Sheriff James Stroud in 2001 to help bring about resolution.

He said he met Hartsfield with a court order in November 2001 and obtained vials of the defendant's blood as well as a statement in which Hartsfield said he had no knowledge of the KFC murders and had never been to the restaurant.

After learning Hartsfield's blood matched the DNA profile on the bloody box, Kieny said he began combing through old evidence again.

Kieny acknowledged under oath he tried for years to tie Mankins to the murders, but was unable to do so.

With Hartsfield as a possible suspect, he found fresh directions to explore.

Kieny was pressed about the origins of the box.

The former FBI agent said he had no personal knowledge of a box containing Hartsfield's DNA coming from the KFC.

"I have not seen an evidence log in the case."

"So," Davidson said, "Is it your opinion that whoever took the victims to that location knew where it was?"

Kieny nodded in agreement.

"Yes it is."

Kieny said he believed he could place Mankins at the scene because he worked for his father, who owned a trucking company that made oil field deliveries, but the evidence was never there.

Officials learned Hartsfield worked in landscaping, construction and with Dillard Exploration, a seismographic company in East Texas, during the 1970s and '80s.

"Did you find anyone else who made oil field deliveries?" Tanner asked.

"Yes. Darnell Hartsfield."

Several jurors looked at the defendant, who began whispering to his attorneys.

Tanner and Jimerson wrapped up about two weeks of testimony with remarks from former Rusk County District Attorney Kyle Freeman on his role in the decades-old case.

Freeman had requested assistance from the Texas Attorney General's Office and was present when Hartsfield testified before a grand jury.

Freeman said the results of DNA testing were known to prosecutors at the time of the grand jury proceedings.

The purpose of having Hartsfield testify was to clarify why his blood may have been in the restaurant, but Hartfield would never admit to being there, he said.

"He told the grand jury, 'That's not my blood,'" Freeman said.

Several jurors looked at Tanner and then at Hartsfield, who was sitting quietly at the table.

A hush swept over the room as Ms. Tanner produced a large stack of papers and manila file folders, 509 pages to be exact.

"I have his medical records," the prosecutor said. "These records include information on an injury he sustained."

"Objection," Killingsworth said. "Those are not records from September 1983 and there is no way of knowing when, in a 12-month period, that injury occurred."

The judge did not immediately respond. Gossett said he wanted to consider the matter before making a ruling.

Jurors took a short recess so he could hear from attorneys

before making a decision. Tanner said the records held important information that could be connected to an injury that happened about the same time as the murders.

"I'm going to allow it." Gossett said a few minutes later.

Tanner said Hartsfield told Texas Ranger Dowell in December 1983 he had not suffered any cuts, but she produced medical records that stated otherwise.

"He told a medical professional in 1999 that he suffered a cut to his right hand in 1983 when he, 'fell on a beer bottle,'" Tanner said. "The cut caused long-term damage to his hand."

Killingsworth and Davidson repeated assertions that the timeline was meaningless.

The state wrapped up its case a short time later.

It was up to the defense to shoot down the case, but it wasn't going to be easy. Tanner and Jimerson introduced more than 140 pieces of evidence and eight days of witness testimony.

The defense started by highlighting inconsistencies in Ranger Dowell's earlier testimony about the discovery of the bloody box.

Dowell said the box was in the office of the restaurant, but Ranger Elliott testified it was found under the front counter.

Davidson and Killingsworth also tried to attack Ranger Elliott's competency as a blood spatter expert.

The defense told jurors no one knew how the blood got on the box recovered from the scene so they were giving the jury alternate theories to think about.

They showed a video shot by private investigator and defense team consultant Vincent "Sonny" Monteagudo that depicted Davidson's legal assistant Katie Baker painting a substance on several white boxes with a makeup brush.

The substance was identified as actual blood, drawn from Killingsworth's arm by a phlebotomist.

Tanner defused the tactic, asking if Monteagudo or Baker were forensic scientists or blood spatter pattern experts.

"No. We were just conducting experiments," Monteagudo said.

Davidson then called Kilgore resident James Rowe, who testified that he was on his way home from his in-laws' home when he noticed a Ford Econoline van take off from the rear of the KFC.

Rowe said the van pulled out in front of him and then skidded to a stop, forcing him to take evasive actions.

"I knew something was going to happen so I took my foot off the accelerator and stopped all of the sudden, and he stopped all of the sudden," Rowe said. "My headlights came about a foot from hitting his door."

Rowe said a white male with long black hair and a shaggy beard was driving the van, and they exchanged stares before the van pulled away.

"We looked at each other right square in the face," Rowe said as he marked where the van and his vehicle stopped.

"Are you sure about what you saw?" Tanner asked.

She referenced grand jury testimony he gave in 2003 and pointed out several points that didn't quite add up: the time at which he left his in-laws' home, where he was going and the purpose of his journey.

On one occasion he said he was going to pick up some snacks for his children, on another, he mentioned they had just finished having cake and ice cream.

Davidson refocused on the key reason Rowe was summoned as a witness.

"Are you sure you saw a white van at the KFC?"

"Yes."

"Are you sure you saw a white man?"

"Yes."

"Are you sure he had a beard?"

"Yes."

Killingsworth also called Irving Stone, former FBI agent and former chief of forensic physical evidence section of the Southwest Institute of Forensic Sciences, who told jurors he tested the fingernail found on Johnson's body and compared it to the fingernails of James Earl Mankins Jr.

Stone said he first believed it was a match.

Tanner, on cross examination, asked if conclusive DNA proved the fingernail did not belong to Mankins, could he accept the findings?

"Assuming it was done correctly and done on the right nail, then yes ma'am," he said.

There was widespread speculation in the 1990s among some in the attorney general's office that the fingernail had been switched to clear Mankins of any involvement in the slayings.

Tanner pressed for a more concrete response.

"This is a slide of that nail," Tanner said, revealing a large-scale photograph of a fingernail fragment. "Was this the nail you tested?"

"Yes, I believe it was," Stone said.

Emotions boiled over in closing arguments when the defense resumed its attacks on the chain of custody of the blood-splattered receipt box.

"If someone secured that box, then where are the contents of the box? Where are the cash register rolls they say were in there?" Killingsworth asked, looking at the jury panel. "We are asking you to take a look at the whole picture. The state is asking you to take a few spots of blood on a box and turn it into murder. That is quite a leap, quite a leap."

Tanner listened to the conjecture, and felt her face burn with anger.

She took the entire 17 minute allocation of time to remind jurors that DNA doesn't lie.

"Despite rabbit trails and rumors, this case is one long robbery that turned very badly," she said. "That's all that it is ... the only five people who could tell us what happened are not with us anymore."

Jurors took less than two hours to reach their conclusion.

Hartsfield stood and faced the jury to await word of his punishment.

Foreman Bradford Smith relayed the jury's finding: Guilty of capital murder.

Hartsfield's eyes remained downcast as Gossett imposed five consecutive life sentences, stacked on top of an earlier life sentence for aggravated perjury in the case.

Family members were given an opportunity to address Hartsfield and explain how they were affected by the murders.

A furious Jack Hughes looked at Hartsfield and said he was disgusted by the lack of emotion displayed during the trial.

He saw arrogance where there should have been remorse.

"For every time you looked back at me and I met your stare

I want you to remember the ... look in my eyes," he said. "I feel for your family. Your family I don't think failed you. You failed your family."

Hughes expressed pity for the two cousins who hurt so many along the way.

"I don't hate you, I feel sorry for you," he said. "I feel sorry for Romeo. I have respect for Romeo because he had the guts to say he was guilty."

Hughes said his hope now is Hartsfield will summon the courage to name the man who raped his precious Opie.

"You cannot imagine, you cannot fathom what these families have been through," he said.

Hartsfield looked away from Hughes' anguished husband, who seemed ready to explode with rage.

"Do you care?" he shouted. "Do you?"

The defendant's gaze returned and silence settled over the courtroom. There was a momentary pause as Hughes took a breath and continued speaking.

"If you do care, then you better get your heart ready with God or you will surely go to hell," he said before returning to his seat.

Kathy Hamilton, Maxwell's sister, told Hartsfield he should be ashamed for hurting so many people, including his own family.

"I have looked at your mama and your sisters sitting here in this courtroom and know that they are hurting too, by your actions that you did," she said. "I hold you responsible for killing my brother. Your actions ruined my family."

Linda Landers said her son, Monte, was an honorable boy who deserved better.

"It took me 10 years to realize that I didn't die," she sobbed. "I had four other children at home ... You know how hard it is to love them, look at them? I can't hold him, but you know sometimes I can still smell him."

She expressed belief that Monte and the others were looking down from the clouds and watching justice unfold.

She was learning to forgive the men responsible for the murders, but like everyone else, she could never forget.

Kimberly Miller issued a written statement about her sadness over the death of her mother, Mary Tyler.

"You have no idea how you have traumatized our lives by your actions. My mama was only 37 years old when you brutally took her life. I just cannot put on paper how much pain you have caused us," the statement read.

Maxwell's widow thanked the jury for listening to the evidence and prosecutors and investigators for their due diligence in seeking closure to the case.

Addressing Hartsfield directly, Lana Maxwell Dunkerley said, "I am sorry because it ruins your family, but it has ruined some of my family more than you will ever know."

The convicted man never spoke, but cast a fleeting look back in the gallery at his heartbroken sister, who sobbed in grief and disbelief.

Jurors shed quiet tears as each victim's name was read into the record.

Emotionally drained, Tanner and Jimerson faced a wall of cameras and journalists after court was adjourned.

"I'm very satisfied, very pleased and very happy for the families," Tanner said, as nearby family members who waited 25 years for closure, sobbed and hugged in apparent celebration.

A short distance away, a defiant Killingsworth was fighting to contain his emotions as he faced the news media.

"Obviously we're disappointed and we were hoping for a better outcome," he said. "The family members want some closure and they want someone convicted and punished. I understand that, but just because they need that, that is not a reason to ignore the lack of evidence against Darnell Hartsfield."

Chapter 22
Faces of the Accused

Angry shouts echo down the halls of the Darrington Unit, one of dozens of prisons managed by the Texas Department of Criminal Justice.

It is early afternoon, but already the temperature outside is starting to rise, igniting tensions inside.

For those housed in the remote, high security prison, there is little escape from the withering Texas heat and the misery it produces.

Some of the state's most dangerous convicts are housed here, men convicted of murder, robbery and rape.

Inmate Darnell Hartsfield, number 01539158, ignores the yelling. He's more focused on seeking relief from the sweaty monotony than figuring out the source of the outburst.

At 55, he's spent more than half his life behind bars, in a cell about the size of a walk-in closet. He has two shelves and a twin-size mattress to call his own, at least for now.

If he leaves this place - whether by transfer, release or coffin - the items will be passed along to the next man.

Hartsfield's fate was sealed after authorities said his DNA was found on a white box inside the restaurant, but he claims he was never there, and he's never stolen a life.

He is aware the cruel nature of the murders continues to inflict misery on those left behind.

"I'm a good person," he said in a 2013 interview with the Tyler Morning Telegraph. "Even though I'm in prison, I've been framed for a crime I didn't commit. I have it on appeal, but I doubt anything will come of it."

Years earlier, at a time when most young men are thinking about chasing women and making money, a much younger Hartsfield was also living the high life.

At 22, he seemed to have it all: fun-loving friends, a knack for sweet talking the ladies and a steady supply of weed.

His exciting, hormone-fueled lifestyle proved a stark contrast to his upbringing.

Hartsfield was one of a handful of children born to John H. Hartsfield and Ruby Mae Pinkerton Hartsfield, who raised their offspring to work hard, tell the truth and make good choices.

They attended church, aided the downtrodden and encouraged their children to move beyond the opportunities offered in Tyler, the Rose Capital.

Hartsfield grew up loving the simple things in life, the taste of his mom's homemade pecan pie, the sounds of laughter at family cookouts and the tantalizing smell of dinner after a long day at school.

"I have a very loving family, very supportive," he said. "I used to work; we had jobs at a real early age. I was always a little mature for my age."

But then the great hormone explosion arrived and he began testing his independence, staying out a little later and hanging out with older teenagers from the neighborhood, including an older teen Hartsfield looked up to and admired.

The activity gained little favor with his folks, especially his mother, who knew that unsupervised teenagers can be a magnet for trouble.

Hartsfield was about 13 when his parents' teachings took second place to the excitement of street life.

"We started hanging out at clubs and smoking weed," he said. "I got a lot of lectures because my mother was a devoted Christian."

In spite of his family's best efforts, Hartsfield said he later stopped attending classes at John Tyler High School and dropped out in the 11th grade, tossing his old life aside to pursue something better, something more stimulating.

An older friend from the neighborhood tried to intervene, but the young man would have none of it.

"He encouraged me not to take that route," Hartsfield said. "But I had found a lifestyle, and the lifestyle I had took root."

The convenience store robbery three days after the murders, which put him squarely in the sights of local police, seemed pivotal to his downfall.

The lone employee at the counter remembered Hartsfield down to the smallest detail.

It seems she was unable to forget the man who aimed a .38 caliber pistol between her eyes for $300 in assorted bills.

Robert Waters' jailhouse ramblings about the KFC murders after the robbery might have stayed private for 18 years, but once the inmate decided to pass that information on to authorities, little time passed before search warrants for his blood were issued.

During a 2013 interview, Hartsfield, serving five life sentences, said he clings to the fantasy of one day being a free man.

"I couldn't do it, I knew I didn't do this crime," he said. "I want people to say I'm innocent ... I have been since day one."

Hartsfield said he took a lie detector test after the murders and passed, but authorities said that's a lie.

He doesn't deny his role in the convenience store robbery or other crimes, saying he smoked a lot of cheap marijuana in those days and didn't make great decisions.

His purpose the night he held up the store clerk was to score a little cash to get more weed, not paint a target on himself as a KFC suspect.

"You look at our records, it was pretty much petty crimes we did," he said. "Even though it was always petty, it didn't lead to what they said I did."

Decades later, the wild, reckless days of his youth are over.

Gone is the youthful swagger. His black, close-cropped hair is flecked with gray; his voice weary. Several teeth are missing.

Most days are spent in the solitude of his cell, reading westerns and philosophy, reflecting on what might have been and preparing his next court filing.

Both parents died during the time he's been locked up; he's also lost half a dozen aunts.

Hartsfield doesn't like discussing how the murders affected those left behind.

"Yes, I have remorse. I think any person in this environment would have... if I could go back, I would," he said. "I sympathize with them (the victims), you know? If they feel like they have closure, it's a false sense."

As for his own family, he said, "They loved me regardless ... They support me even now. When times get hard, I would think of my family."

He remembers the day authorities questioned him about the murders.

"They pretty much knew me, my character," he said. "They were examining me for cuts ... they didn't find any. They didn't believe I did it. I was dropped as a person of interest. I knew I was innocent of it."

Hartsfield said he's not surprised about the guilty verdict in his capital murder trial.

Coming from a poor black family, he said there was not enough money to hire a good attorney.

"I felt like it was going to happen," he said. "He never came to (visit me in) prison. I took that as a sign. I think the attorney general is applying a lot of pressure. Yes, I'm angry about it, very upset. I have to keep on living, keep on fighting for my innocence."

Pinkerton, who turned 56 in 2014, doesn't like to talk about his life, his role in the murders or how he was linked to KFC, although authorities said DNA was the key to sealing his fate.

He is serving five life sentences after pleading guilty in 2007, to avoid receiving the death penalty and to escape the

Bowie County Jail, where he felt threatened.

Pinkerton refuses most interviews.

In a brief interview with the Tyler Morning Telegraph after his trial, Pinkerton was quick to claim his innocence.

"I didn't do this," he said. "I only said that I did to avoid the death penalty. That's all I have to say."

In a 2009 interview with the Associated Press from the Robertson Unit of the Texas Department of Criminal Justice, he again denied playing a role in the slayings, saying he's behind bars because of race not evidence.

"The real killer is out there still walking around," he said. "I'm innocent all day long in this case. I never took anybody's life."

Pinkerton calls the evidence against him a conspiracy.

Jimerson, the Rusk County district attorney who helped Tanner prosecute the case, said he doesn't buy Pinkerton's claims of innocence because DNA doesn't lie.

It's unrealistic to assume police, before the advent of DNA testing, recognized the significance of that blood smear, Jimerson said.

The DA's position on Pinkerton's guilt is accepted by Griffith, one of the convicted man's trial lawyers.

"You would have to have somebody planting evidence roughly five years before DNA became useful as a forensic tool," Griffith told the Associated Press. "That would be like somebody planting evidence of ballistics five years before guns were invented."

Former oil field worker James Mankins, Jr., in some respects, is still viewed by some as one of the most infamous mass murderers in Texas history, yet he was never tried or convicted of the crimes.

Mankins said he told Kieny, Dowell and other investigators all along he wasn't the guy.

History suggests there may be people out there who still and will always believe Mankins is responsible, even with DNA pinpointing Hartsfield, Pinkerton and a third man as the people responsible for the killings.

In a 2003 interview from the Federal Correction Institution in Texarkana, Mankins said his name may always be linked to the crime because of public opinion, in spite of what the evidence says.

"I've lived with this so long," he said. "I'll be a suspect for the rest of my life."

Investigators once believed enough evidence existed in the early days of the case to support an indictment and conviction, but as it stands today, there are no witnesses, no DNA and no firearm putting Mankins at the scene.

Authorities were so convinced Mankins was involved in the homicides, they placed a snitch in his cell to see if he would do what many inmates do... talk about their crimes to bolster their credibility in prison.

He never did.

Portions of Mankins' records have since been expunged to remove any reference of the capital murder indictments.

After prolonged scrutiny over Mankins' presumed guilt or innocence, there is no escaping the obvious — years of confinement and stress have taken their toll.

The shaggy, unkempt hair and cocky swagger captured in grainy television footage and yellowing newspaper articles is gone. The image of a young dope-dealing thug has been replaced by that of a middle-aged man with gray hair and bifocals.

He's in his 60s now and a grandfather.

"I'm tired," he said.

In letters sent to the Tyler Morning Telegraph, Mankins said he worked hard in prison to stay out of trouble, providing as proof copies of his work program reviews, which indicate clear conduct and outstanding job performance.

The aging former outlaw said his family experienced undue hardship due to his past mistakes, and he doesn't want another generation to live under the same cloud of suspicion.

He was successful in having his records expunged so his grandchildren can see him as someone different than his persona in the news media.

"I accept a lot," he said in 2003. "I know how things are. I don't know who did it, but if I did, I would have told them about it 20 years ago."

Epilogue

David Maxwell's widow, Lana Maxwell Dunkerley, doesn't like to discuss the murders, but she consents to interviews because it helps keep his memory alive. Dunkerley spent her adulthood trying to be strong for herself and her son.

Little things can still spark concern - her third husband, Bill, running late or one of the kids forgetting to return a message - but she's learning to control the anxiety.

It took 24 years to bring the first killer to justice and Dunkerley says she's not waiting around for another trial to enjoy life again.

She is happy for the first time in years, thanks to years of counseling and a supportive husband.

Her dream is to retire to the Texas Hill Country and open a little quilting shop.

She said Hartsfield and Pinkerton's convictions have brought some relief to decades of pain.

"I can honestly say I'm happy," she said. "There are no ghosts here. I will upset people when I say this, but I really have forgiven those men. Every one of us has the same ability to sin ... and they, unfortunately, were forgotten somewhere in their lives."

A devout Christian, Dunkerly said she pities and prays for the convicted men, especially Pinkerton who didn't seem to have any family in court supporting him.

"I would look at him in court," she said. "He would turn around, look and start rocking. When he was rocking, you knew something was going on in his head. He was trying to be all mean, but all I could see was a little boy who had no one to hug and kiss him ... nobody loved him and nobody cared for him."

She was saddened and relieved when he pleaded guilty.

"I felt so sorry for him," she said. "I was really proud of him. It took a lot of courage to own it. I don't think his heart was so rock hard that the Lord couldn't reach him. I'm not angry anymore; I just want to know what happened."

***

Mary Tyler's stepdaughter, Denise Maynard, who was just a child when the murders were committed, said she never stopped missing her stepmom.

Maynard couldn't speak in person about the loss, but did agree to share a poem she wrote in 1991 on the anniversary of the slayings.

She put pen to paper as a way to pay tribute to the friendly, bubbly woman who brought a certain warmth to the family home.

"Good-Bye"
It seemed to us, just a regular day,
And we never thought it would end this way;
The day seemed to go by pretty fast,
And no one could have guessed it being your last;
The night came, and we said good night,
The last thing I remember was the disappearance of your car headlights;
There has not been a day that hasn't gone by,
That I haven't asked myself. 'Why?'

157

Ever since that day, you've been in our hearts, and on our minds,
The place you'll be for ALL time!
I miss you.

Maynard hopes her stepmother will always be remembered as a kind and generous soul, not a murder victim.

***

Joey Johnson's girlfriend, Leona Dorsey Johnson Tripp, whose letter was discovered in the restaurant, believes her life would have been a lot different had her first love survived.

She went on to love again after he was murdered, falling for his older brother, Jimmy.

The couple had two beautiful children together, the first arriving before she finished high school. He spent time in prison, twice, but they managed to stay together 20 years before divorcing, she said.

"We went through Heaven and hell together until the day he died of cancer a few years ago," she said. "We divorced before he got sick, but stayed the closest of friends."

She wonders what life might have been like, had she become Mrs. Joey Johnson. She believes she might have finished college, developed a professional career and never started smoking.

Today, she's again happily married and remains close with members of the Johnson family, who did not wish to be interviewed about their loss.

"I'm proud of who I am today and I love the life I'm living," she said.

Tripp adores her husband, children and grandchildren, but every September she feels a pang of sadness for the funny boy with the curly red hair and clear blue eyes.

She sometimes runs across a copy of that letter penned so long ago in Mrs. McCathran's English class and wonders what might have been.

"My life would have been a lot different," she said. "The world lost a jewel when it lost Joey."

***

Rusk County property owners Keri and Dale Duke live in a tidy brick home off Walker King Road, a few feet away from where the bodies of the five victims were found more than three decades ago.

They purchased the home several years ago because they liked it, not because of the historic significance of the now grassy field a stone's throw away from their two-car garage.

"I suspected this was the place," she said. "I do remember the murders, I was very young, about seven and in the first grade. I know it's been a big deal around here since then."

The once remote location is much less remote these days.

The thicket of briars is gone, replaced by golden blades of native grasses. Along with the brick home, there is a barn and an updated metal gate protecting the location from trespassers. The old gate, perhaps the exact one standing at the time of the murders, lays nearby.

There are neighboring homes with gardens, mooing cattle nibbling at hay and rattling school buses delivering children.

The road still doesn't get an abundance of traffic, but there are occasional vehicles that seem to slow as they pass, especially around Sept. 23 of every year.

"My husband had never heard about the murders, he didn't grow up around here," Duke said. "It doesn't bother me to be here, I'm not scared or anything. It's just home."

***

Former Kilgore Police Investigator Danny Pirtle went on to serve as sheriff of Rusk County, the same entity he battled so many years ago.

His days are spent enjoying the peace and solitude that comes with living lakeside in a tidy, modest home he built by hand over a span of nine years.

Looking out over the water as it laps at his boat dock, Pirtle describes his love for his wife, Dolly, a fiery Italian, who holds his heart and the key to his happiness. They met after he served her with divorce papers and they've been happily married for 33 years.

"Talk about your first meetings," he said laughing.

Their three boys are all grown up and in 2013, the couple welcomed another grandchild. Dolly adores gardening. The retired lawman is a fisherman.

Pirtle didn't grow up dreaming of being in law enforcement, he just liked the idea of helping people.

The walls of his office "man cave" are blanketed in photographs of various officers and memorable cases solved along the way, though there is no sign of KFC.

"It's been a good career, I'm going to miss it," he said.

He's battled a series of health issues in recent years that prompted him to take a fresh look at his life and what it's all meant. He appreciates life more these days and simple pleasures of watching the grandchildren dog paddle around his fishing pier.

Like those who gave up family members in KFC, Pirtle said he and the others who fought for years to resolve the case, lost out too. Too many ball games missed, too many nights there was an empty seat at the dinner table.

He still thinks of the case and still has nightmares about what might have been missed along the way.

"It took a lot from me," he said. "I had a son that was several years behind the other two. He needed me then. He understood I had a job to do. I knew I had a job to do and I did it … yes, there were many days that I didn't think we would ever get it solved. Thinking about it at night would literally choke me."

***

Texas prosecutor Lisa Tanner is still with the Attorney General's Office, probing new cases in hopes of bringing closure to other victims.

She still responds to appeals filed by Hartsfield and Pinkerton and checks out occasional leads that could identify the third suspect.

Relatives of the KFC victims still call to say hello and issue an invite for her stop in sometime.

Tanner's office is clear of the dozens of cardboard boxes containing of KFC files; they have been moved to a storage room just down the hall.

She keeps a less obvious sign of her career case taped to her office door: A scrap of paper from a fortune cookie that reads, "No one conquers who doesn't fight."

She keeps it as a permanent reminder of the many late night KFC strategy meetings held before the trials and a symbol of what can happen when people refuse to give up.

Tanner said the case was wrought with problems from the onset: too many hands in the investigation, too many jurisdictions and too many incorrect assumptions.

On and on it goes, creating a perfect storm of challenges: No weapons located; crime scenes compromised; chains of custody broken; evidence lost or destroyed.

"It was a mess," she said in a 2013 interview. "I did not know, until I took over the case, how screwed up the DNA was until I started looking at it."

She's still haunted by the memory of informing the victims' families the fingernail did not belong to Mankins.

"It was horrible," she said. "I had to tell them that, what they had believed for years, was wrong … I'll never forget it as long as I live."

She looks forward to the day when the final suspect will be identified. Only then, can she move on.

"It was the biggest case I've ever had and the biggest case I ever will have," Tanner said. "It's been there almost my entire career. KFC is my baby and it always will be my baby. Without question, it's very, very, very, very special to me."

In spite of the convictions, there are some people who still wonder how a couple of small town criminals could kidnap five people at gunpoint, corral them into a getaway vehicle on a busy Friday night and kill them in a remote oil field 18 miles away in less than an hour, without someone noticing.

***

Ranger Stuart Dowell, in one of his last interviews before his 2006 death, said he would always believe there was something far more sinister at play than an ordinary robbery.

He went to his grave believing the killings were the work of a drug ring, who thought a special recipe for making methamphetamine was stashed in the restaurant and the robbers were retaliating.

Were he alive today, he would be waiting for the arrest of the third suspect.

Authorities believe that third person may be dead, but no one has come forward to say for certain.

Until that person is identified, one of Texas' longest unresolved mass murder cases shall remain open.

***

Tyler Morning Telegraph Publisher Nelson Clyde IV said his newspaper will continue to monitor the case should new developments arise, no matter how long it takes.

"We can't rest until the story is finished, that's our responsibility," he said. "We need to be respectful of the people and the tragedies that affect their lives."

Clyde believes keeping the story alive could compel someone to step forward with a tidbit of information that could close a painful chapter in the lives of many East Texans.

He's hoping that closure comes on his watch.

"You never know," he said. "We need to believe it could happen."

***

Texan prison inmates Darnell Hartsfield and Romeo Pinkerton both filed motions asking for their DNA to be retested, but Gossett, the judge presiding over their cases, struck down the requests, saying several labs, including one hired by the men's attorneys, already completed them with no change in the results.

Pinkerton was scheduled for a parole hearing in 2014, but victims' families rallied and sent letters asking that he remain behind bars. He was denied release.

***

Rusk County District Attorney Micheal Jimerson said the Kilgore community seems to be showing signs of recovery.

"Before, it was almost constant, everyone had a KFC story," he said in a 2014 interview with the newspaper. "It was so shocking, you can't even wrap your mind around five dead. Before, everybody talked about it … I think it's starting to die down a bit now."

He still sees family and friends of the victims around town, as well as long-term players in the investigation. The hurt is still there, but the convictions seem to help with the healing.

"You don't pray for the big cases, not in this business," he said. "You give up a lot of your life to do this, it never leaves your mind … it's good to get it behind us as a community."

Jimerson doesn't try to claim political credit for the convictions, saying KFC will always be Tanner's case. He inherited the opportunity to participate in it from his predecessor Freeman, whom he describes as a respectable gentleman with a good heart.

The DA's greatest satisfaction these days comes from attending ball games and Cub Scout meetings with his young son and spending time with his wife, Mona.

Looking back, Jimerson said he's confident the jury would have passed a death penalty sentence against Pinkerton, but he suspects it might have been overturned later in an appeals court.

"We had evidence placing them in the KFC, but nothing tying them to the murder scene," he said. "All we had on that was a cellmate telling us that Romeo made a gun gesture pulling the trigger as it related to news about the case. We did not have any weapons or anyone who could place them at the scene."

Evidence in the restaurant proved critical to gaining convictions.

He and others suspect if the Pinkerton case had gone to a jury, he might have walked.

"I truly believe we have the right people behind bars, but this was a weak homicide case in that we just didn't have anything putting them at the place where the bodies were found," he said.

He doesn't believe Pinkerton, given his criminal history, will be successful in convincing the parole board he deserves freedom.

***

Rusk County Investigator William Brown retired in 2015, but he is not holding his breath the fine details of the case will ever be revealed.

Brown moved on to other cases, after the murders, but the memories of the KFC slayings went with him.

He grimaces when discussing the complexity of solving the restaurant murders and the countless hours spent chasing unproductive leads.

Brown and others suspect the third person is dead and may never be revealed, no matter how long they search.

"There is a third person, based on what we know," Brown said. "In my opinion, we have the right people. Are we ever going to know what happened? I personally don't believe so."

***

J.B Smith, the retired silver-haired sheriff of Smith County, Texas, isn't comfortable talking about the KFC murder investigation and its many twists, although the crime happened in a neighboring jurisdiction and he makes a respectable living as an Emmy Award-winning entertainer.

In his public persona, Smith is exactly what one might expect to find in a Texas sheriff – expensive leather boots, big cowboy hat and shiny belt-buckle so large it could rival a small dinner plate.

He is a comical story-teller, a polished politician and tireless philanthropist.

Smith routinely shows up at funerals to comfort the bereaved and visits assisted living centers to cheer the aging.

Ailing constituents are sometimes surprised when he appears at the hospital door with a unique kind of cure: single servings of warm red beans and yellow corn bread.

All this hand-shaking, meal sharing and hugging provides Smith with rare, personal glimpses into the lives and loves of area residents.

Consequently, he's in the know on just about everybody and everything going on in Smith County.

So it came as a complete surprise that fateful morning in 1983 the sheriff's phone wasn't ringing after five bodies were discovered.

"I tell you, it was the damnedest thing," Smith said during a December 2014 interview. "They cut me out, I couldn't find out anything."

It appeared professional courtesies – alerting neighboring agencies of unfolding murder investigations - were nowhere to be found it seemed, so Smith decided to offer his support.

"I can remember calling Kilgore PD and Tyler and saying, 'If there's anything you need, just let me know,'" he said. "We were concerned. This happened in the next county, little more than 30 miles away from my office."

It is – and was - common knowledge among lawmen if you want to learn the juicy details of a crime, a visit with Smith County Jail inmates is time well spent.

"I had one of the highest clearance of cases in the state of Texas," Smith said. "I found all the information I needed from the Smith County Jail. We had a wealth of information in our jail."

Yet no one with authority over the KFC investigation seemed interested, he said.

"We never understood why," Smith said. "The inmates know we can put in a good word for them or a bad word. When these guys are going to trial, they'll talk. They don't care, they would turn in their own mother if it benefits them."

The former sheriff could not recall any early instances in which KFC murder investigators sought jailhouse visits with inmates or offered updates on possible developments.

"Everything I got was out of the newspaper, I had nothing else," Smith said, shaking his head. "It didn't have to be that way. It was a common sense thing for law enforcement to get all the agencies together and talk about these things. Unfortunately, anytime you have multiple agencies involved in anything and you're dealing with a lot of egos from multiple departments, you have a problem... It appeared to us that nobody was getting along."

Smith said he will always have questions about the case.

He found it interesting the state collected DNA samples from close to 200 men to locate a suspect. Most murder investigations that include DNA testing focus on a smaller pool of suspects, maybe five or six people.

"I've had my nose broken, I've been shot at and stabbed, but I've never, ever been assaulted by someone smoking dope," he said. "Drunks yes, but I've never dealt with anybody violent on pot, at least not me personally."

Equally mystifying, he added, is the fact that for more than 30 years neither man bragged or fessed up to the killings.

People trying to survive confinement typically talk about their crimes to establish credibility among others, he said.

"Considering the personalities of criminals in general, and considering the type of criminals they are, I'm surprised they've never said anything," Smith said.

He believes the spirit of cooperation among East Texas law enforcement agencies is greatly improved since the KFC murders, and he hopes the lessons learned from the experience will not be forgotten.

"It's just so sad," Smith said. "That crime could have been solved a lot sooner, but wasn't because of non-communication between agencies. The days of the Lone Ranger are over."

***

There are many people who believe the identity of the third suspect will remain a mystery forever.

Statistically, the odds of finding the individual do not appear favorable, assuming his chronological age is about the same as the two men convicted of the murders.

The average life expectancy of an African-American male born in 1960 is about 58 years, according to the United States Centers for Disease Control and Prevention.

Certain risk factors, such as participation in criminal acts and substance abuse, could also affect someone's life span, the agency reports.

The Kilgore KFC Murder case will remain open until authorities learn more about the unknown culprit, who had contact with Mrs. Hughes in her last hours.

Anyone with information about the third person, dead or alive, is urged to contact authorities and the Tyler Morning Telegraph.

Family members of the victims, who have endured decades of suffering, deserve answers.

Timeline

Sept. 23, 1983
Working at the Kentucky Fried Chicken restaurant in Kilgore
are Mary Tyler, 37, Opie Hughes, 39, and Joey Johnson, 20.
David Maxwell, 20, an off-duty employee, and Monte Landers, 19, are visiting Johnson. At about 11 p.m., Mrs. Tyler's
daughter, Kim, arrives. A door is open and blood is on the
floor.

Sept. 24, 1983
An oil field worker arriving about 9 a.m. at a well in Rusk
County finds the five victims. Each had been shot in the back
of the head.

Sept. 26, 1983
Preliminary autopsy reports indicate more than one gun may
have been used.

Sept. 28, 1983
DPS appoints Texas Ranger Capt. G.W. Burks of Dallas to co-ordinate the investigation after law officers in Rusk and Gregg counties complain cooperation is breaking down.

March 7, 1995
A Rusk County grand jury begins hearing KFC testimony.

April 27, 1995
The grand jury indicts James Earl Mankins Jr. on five counts of capital murder. Investigators say a fingernail recovered from the clothing of one of the victims matches a torn nail on Mankins' hand.

June 26, 1995
Court papers reveal a napkin with bloodstains from an un-identified source was recovered from the restaurant during the initial investigation.

Nov. 13, 1995
A judge drops capital murder charges against Mankins after more tests establish the fingernail did not belong to him.

Feb. 22, 2002
Rusk County Sheriff James Stroud says blood samples from a possible suspect will be compared to crime-scene evidence.

Aug. 19, 2002
Sources tell the Tyler Morning Telegraph that tests matching DNA to crime-scene blood link two suspects to the murders.

Aug. 21, 2002
Texas Attorney General's Office confirms it will assist in securing indictments against and ultimately prosecuting sus-pects.

Aug. 29, 2002
The Rusk County district attorney seeks prosecution assistance from the Texas Attorney General's Office.

May 8, 2003
A judge orders references to Mankins' indictments in the case be expunged from records.

Sept. 8, 2003
A new grand jury in Rusk begins hearing KFC evidence.

Nov. 10, 2004
A Rusk County grand jury indicts Darnell Hartsfield on aggravated perjury charges for allegedly lying about being in the KFC restaurant.

July 30, 2005
Romeo Pinkerton is arrested in Tyler on charges of burglarizing Griffin Elementary School and evading arrest/detention.

Oct. 9, 2005
Several lawmen familiar with the case tell the Tyler Morning Telegraph they believe there is enough evidence to solve the case.

Oct. 26, 2005
A jury finds Darnell Hartsfield guilty of aggravated perjury for lying to a grand jury investigating the KFC case. He said he was not in the restaurant, but DNA indicated he was present.

Nov. 17, 2005
Texas Attorney General Greg Abbott announces a grand jury has indicted Darnell Hartsfield and Romeo Pinkerton each on five counts of capital murder.

Aug. 6, 2007

Jury selection begins in the capital murder case against Romeo Pinkerton.

Oct. 15, 2007
Opening arguments begin in New Boston in the capital murder case against Pinkerton.

Oct. 29, 2007
Romeo Pinkerton pleads guilty to five counts of murder, avoiding the death penalty of a capital murder conviction. He receives five life sentences.

Sept. 9, 2008
Jury selection in the case against Darnell Hartsfield begins in Bryan, Texas.

Oct. 1, 2008
Darnell Hartsfield is found guilty of five counts of capital murder. He receives five life sentences.

Oct. 22, 2009
Darnell Hartsfield files an appeal in the conviction.

Feb. 5, 2010
Darnell Hartsfield's conviction in the capital murder cases is upheld by the Sixth Court of Appeals.

Sept. 7, 2012
Romeo Pinkerton and Darnell Hartsfield's request for new DNA testing in the case was denied by 4th District Judge Clay Gossett, Jr.

Present
Authorities continue searching for the presumed third killer in the case.

Notes on Sources

Jacque Hilburn-Simmons and Kenneth Dean have each spent years covering developments in the KFC murders. Here, the journalists share their thoughts as they reflect on the case that became a centerpiece of their careers.

***

It was Tyler Morning Telegraph editor and author Roy Maynard, who first suggested the KFC murders was a topic worthy of its own book.

Roy is an accomplished author with myriad books to his credit, including a "whodunit" detective series used today for classroom study and debate.

At the time of our 2012 brainstorming meeting about possible book topics, almost 30 years had passed since the slayings and the subject had been explored in detail in the pages of the newspaper.

Ever the skeptic, I asked a two-fold question: Do you believe there is anything new to discover about the case and will people be at all interested?

His answer to both questions was the same: "Definitely."

I decided if a book was to be written about KFC, it would not be complete without the assistance of longtime colleague Kenneth Dean, who has covered the case for years and maintains close ties with key players in the case.

We've worked together on hot issue stories for more than 10 years and agreed to partner up on this project, which amounted to the largest of our careers.

By September 2012, we presented a proposal and outline to the newspaper's management. Our goal was to explore the murders from a variety of perspectives, including our own as journalists. Gratefully, Nelson Clyde IV, whose father led the charge for so many years to keep the case in the headlines, was supportive of the venture.

Our first steps carried us straight to the newspaper's massive collection of archives, which included the much coveted "black binder" that contained old records dating back to the early hours of the investigation.

I remembered the black binder from my early days with the newspaper. Nelson Clyde III was its caretaker, and he revealed it with great reverence to a small group of us entrusted in 2002 to reveal that suspects in the cold murder case had been identified through DNA.

What I didn't know then, as a relative newcomer to East Texas, was how deeply the components of the case still reverberated with the locals. People who lived in the region at that time remembered the crime and the victims and the pain and the terror.

I didn't have those same connections, having grown up in Hunt County, but I was the same age as the three students killed and remembered hearing about their deaths while attending college in Commerce. Like so many other families, my parents told me to stay on campus and avoid being out after nightfall.

After that first meeting with Nelson Clyde III, I knew the story of KFC was extraordinary on many levels and deserving of our best efforts as journalists to keep it alive.

As part of that early coverage, I visited James Earl Mankins, Jr. in federal prison to glean his thoughts on the case. Interviews with other inmates who knew Romeo Pinkerton and Darnell Hartsfield soon followed, but it was Mankins who, for a time, stayed in touch.

He followed up our interview with a series of letters, always reiterating his innocence and insisting authorities lost valuable time by focusing on him instead of other possible suspects. He declined to participate in this book project, so we used excerpts of his letters to help round out his character.

When my work responsibilities at the newspaper changed, Kenneth was charged with watchdogging the developments. Over the years, he's interviewed dozens of people connected with the case and sat through endless hours of courtroom testimony as charges in the mass murder case slowly wound its way through the justice system.

Those experiences allowed us to retell the drama and heartache that played out in the courtroom and other parts of the narrative.

Our 2013 interview with Darnell Hartsfield was insightful and chilling. He was very open about how hard his parents worked to provide for the family. He was still a boy when he chose to turn his back on those early Christian teachings and pursue a different lifestyle, filled with drug use and lawless behavior.

Hartsfield said he looks back on those days with a mixture of emotions, mostly frustration over the fact that his life might be very different today had he only listened to his parents.

We believe Hartsfield knows the identity of the third suspect identified by DNA. We also believe that person is dead.

When asked if Hartsfield thought we would see another person identified or convicted of the murders in our lifetime, his face seemed to fall and there was an obvious tone of sadness in his response.

"No," he said, shaking his head. "I don't see it."

Was the third suspect killed to encourage his silence? Are

there others out there who threatened the lives of Hartsfield and Pinkerton if they revealed what happened that night?

We've batted around those theories to the point of exhaustion, but the only people who know the actual truth aren't telling, at least as of the publishing of this manuscript.

Pinkerton declined to participate in the book project so we took comments from a brief interview he had with Kenneth several years earlier.

Compiling new and old data was a monumental task, which involved combing through files of tattered newspaper clippings and years of electronic archives. It was inspiring to see how our former colleagues really took this story to heart and brought it to life for readers.

The amount of information gathered was so extensive, we opted to divide the responsibilities - Kenneth completed most of the interviews and investigation while I tackled the bulk of the compilation and writing.

It took the better part of a year to weave it all together.

Along the way, Kenneth reached out to surviving family members to see if they wanted to share stories of their lives and how they were changed by the murders.

Some relatives wanted to talk, but were simply too weary to reopen old wounds and chose to forgo additional interviews. Some submitted their thoughts in writing so as to create a buffer between their pain and our curiosity.

Others welcomed us into their homes and places of their choosing.

The resulting interviews were astounding and humbling, and I was deeply moved by their words.

Through their memories, the five victims essentially came to life in my mind. Not merely names repeated over and over in the newspaper, but real moms and college guys with families who loved them. I grieved for the potential that was lost and will never be realized.

Perhaps most surprising to me, personally, was seeing the fresh, raw, pain in the hearts of those left behind, as though no time had passed at all.

I think Nelson Clyde III would be pleased that the story he cared about so much is still alive and in the headlines, so long as the third suspect goes unnamed.

We would be wrong to allow readers to believe this book is the result of just a few people at work.

In reality, the newspaper's accounting of the KFC murders is the result of decades of contributions from reporters, photographers, copy editors, designers, press room employees, carriers and other professionals.

Among them: Nelson Clyde III, Nelson Clyde IV, Roy Maynard, Danny Mogle, Dave Berry, Jim Giametta, Lew K. Cohn, Marvin Ellis, Laura Honeycutt, Wayne Roper, Doug Cosper, Tres Watson, Marilyn Covey, Donna Lestage, Rob Moritz, Mike Cochran, Shauna Wonzer and Gary Lynch.

A special word of thanks is extended to editors Richard Loomis and daughter, Melissa Loomis Wagner, for coaching us through the final leg of this project.

For their efforts, as well as the many others, we are most grateful and appreciative.

-Jacque Hilburn-Simmons

***

This case has always struck a personal chord with me. I was in high school in Tyler at the time and remember how shocking the murders were to everyone here in East Texas.

On the night of Sept. 23, 1983, I was at the East Texas State Fair with a group of friends from Robert E. Lee High School, enjoying the midway and, of course, the fair food.

Little did we know as we laughed and rode on the carnival rides, less than 30 miles down the road five people were about to lose their lives.

The KFC murders dominated the news on TV and the newspaper over the next several days and a panic seemed to spread throughout the area.

People were asking, "Who were the killers and would they strike again?"

As the questions continued to circulate, Tyler Independent School District officials decided to temporarily suspend all off-campus lunches for students.

They could not guarantee our safety at the pizza joint in Broadway Square Mall.

As the years passed, I would go on to graduate. I soon moved away, married and had three daughters.

From time to time the murders would cross my mind, but as with most things in life, time does cause the memory to fade.

I returned to the area and joined the staff of the Tyler Morning Telegraph in May of 2001, not realizing that two years later I would be assigned to the case that left such an impression those many years ago.

I was nervous the day Nelson Clyde III called me into his office.

He said a special grand jury in Rusk County was about to hear testimony in the KFC case.

He instructed me to watch the courts, talk with sources and take note of every person who walked in and out of the grand jury room.

His parting words that day left a lasting impression.

"I can't stress the importance of this story to this newspaper," he said.

I spent the next few months sitting on a bench, watching people come and go.

That's how I met Lisa Tanner, the young and confident prosecutor for the attorney general's office and her investigators.

Tanner didn't like me much at the beginning, especially after I penned a story saying the AG's office had egg on its face after the Mankins' debacle.

As the weeks and months passed, Tanner and I kept running into each other at the courthouse.

One day, she mentioned liking a story I had written for the day's paper.

I felt really good about our coverage and commitment to the story.

Rusk County District Attorney Micheal Jimerson and his staff, were always helpful, especially William Brown, who was never caught outside without his trademark cowboy hat.

William became a great ally over the years and I think he might have helped smooth over the rough patches with Tanner and the AG's office.

I sat through three trials and got to know many people associated with the case, including Tanner, family members and investigators.

When Jacque and I went to Austin in 2013 to interview Tanner, she greeted me with a hug instead of a frown.

With most stories, a journalist writes what happened and then moves on to the next, but the KFC case will forever be intertwined with my career.

I learned how to gain the trust of the families, the accused, the defense teams, the cops and the prosecutors.

The mystery surrounding all of the details of the case may never be solved, but many of us will always be watching for the latest development in the case.

-Kenneth Dean

Sources

Ancestry.com

Autopsy Exam reports, Southwest Institute of Forensic Sciences, Sept. 25, 1983

East Texas Oilfield Museum online archives

Findagrave.com

Houston Chronicle, Aug. 25, 2007; April 17, 2009

Interviews with Arthur Warlick, 2002, 2003; James Stroud; 2002; Gregory Eugene Muse, August 2003; James Earl Mankins Jr., January 2003; George Kieny, 2005; Stuart Dowell, 2005; Glenn Elliott, 2005; Lorna Beasley, September 2007; Manuel Valadez, September 2007; James Nichols, September 2007; Romeo Pinkerton, 2009; William Brown, August 2013, September 2013, October 2014; Danny Pirtle, August 2013, September 2013, October 2014; Lana Maxwell Dunkerley, August 2013; Darnell Hartsfield, August 2013; Kersti Nicholson, September 2013; Lisa Tanner, June 2013, 2014; Leona Dorsey Johnson Tripp, August 2014; Micheal Jimerson, Aug. 29, 2014, October 2014; Keri Duke, September 2013. Conversations also held with R. Daryll Bennett, Jack

Hughes, James Mankins Sr. and Misty Wolfe.
Letters from James E. Mankins Jr. February 2003 – May 2003
Letter from James E. Mankins, Sr., July 15, 2003
Media Advisory, Texas Attorney General's Office, Nov. 13, 1985
Media Advisory, Rusk County Sheriff's Office, Aug. 22 and 23, 2002
Obituary for James Earl Mankins, Sr. , Rader Funeral Home, Kilgore, Texas, Aug. 20, 2013
Obituary for Ruby Mae Pinkerton Hartsfield, Tyler Morning Telegraph, Feb. 27, 2009
Obituary for Stuart Dowell, Texas Ranger Hall of Fame and Museum, 2009, taken from Tyler Morning Telegraph, May 17, 2006
Personal Courtroom Observations, October 2005; October 2007; October 2008
Subpoena from Rusk County for notes of Jacque Hilburn, Sept. 16, 2003
Texas State Historical Association archives
Tyler Morning Telegraph, in order of appearance in manuscript: April 25, 1995; Sept. 24, 1988; Oct. 9, 2005; March 8, 1995; September 25, 1983; March 8, 1995; Sept. 25, 198; Oct. 7, 1983; Oct. 8, 1983; Oct. 9, 1983; Sept. 30, 1983; Sept. 26, 1983; Sept. 27, 1983; Sept. 29, 1983; Sept. 23, 1985; Sept. 24, 1985; Nov. 20, 1994; Nov. 2, 1983; Oct. 1, 1983; March 10, 1985; Dec. 7, 1995; June 18, 1995; June 25, 1995; May 12, 1995; April 28, 1995; June 30, 1995; March 6, 1995; July 11, 1995; March 8, 1995; March 10, 1995; June 24, 1995; March 4, 1995; March 10, 1995; Nov. 15, 1990; Jan. 12, 2004; Aug. 19, 1995; April 28, 1995; Sept. 23, 1989; Aug. 20, 2002; Aug. 21, 2002; Sept. 23, 1987; Sept. 25, 1988; Oct. 2, 1983; Aug. 22, 2003; Dec. 21, 2001; Dec. 21, 2001; Aug. 22, 2002; May 2006; Oct. 9, 2005; Feb. 3, 2004; October 2007; Oct. 8, 1983; Oct. 11, 1983
Voluntary Statement to Police, Kimberly Miller, Sept. 24, 1983

In a surprise move, the Tyler Morning Telegraph featured a front page photo of the bodies on Sept. 23, 1984, a year after the murders. Publisher Nelson Clyde wanted to revive interest in solving the case. The newspaper ran the photo again several years later.

KFC Trial – Then defendant Romeo Pinkerton is flanked by his attorney during his 2007 trial in Bowie County.

A cold locker in the crime lab of the Texas Department of Public Safety in Garland, Texas, was home to KFC evidence for more than 20 years.

Former Texas Attorney General Greg Abbott holds a press conference in 2005 at the Rusk County Courthouse in Henderson to announce developments in the case.

Fourth District Judge Clay Gossett speaks to the news media about the case and courtroom etiquette.

Opie Hughes   *Joey Johnson*   *Monte Landers*   *David Maxwell*   *Mary Tyler*

Oil field worker Arthur Warlick recalls the day he stumbled on the bodies while checking drilling equipment. The remarks were published in a 2004 news story.

Prosecutor Lisa Tanner, Texas Attorney General's Office, shares her memories of preparing and trying the case.

Darnell Hartsfield, at left, on trial in 2005 for perjury in Rusk County, is escorted to the courthouse from the jail by a deputy.

Tyler Morning Telegraph Publisher Nelson Clyde talks in a 2013 interview about his father's resolve to keep the old murder case in the headlines until it was solved.

Lana Dunkerley talks about her late husband, David Maxwell, who was one of the victims found dead in the oil field.

Made in the USA
Middletown, DE
06 January 2022

57938903R00109